Cambridge Elements

Elements in Generative AI in Education
edited by
Mark Warschauer
University of California, Irvine
Tamara Tate
University of California, Irvine

GENERATIVE ARTIFICIAL INTELLIGENCE AND LANGUAGE TEACHING

Benjamin Luke Moorhouse
City University of Hong Kong

Kevin M. Wong
Pepperdine University

Shaftesbury Road, Cambridge CB2 8EA, United Kingdom

One Liberty Plaza, 20th Floor, New York, NY 10006, USA

477 Williamstown Road, Port Melbourne, VIC 3207, Australia

314–321, 3rd Floor, Plot 3, Splendor Forum, Jasola District Centre, New Delhi – 110025, India

103 Penang Road, #05–06/07, Visioncrest Commercial, Singapore 238467

Cambridge University Press is part of Cambridge University Press & Assessment, a department of the University of Cambridge.

We share the University's mission to contribute to society through the pursuit of education, learning and research at the highest international levels of excellence.

www.cambridge.org
Information on this title: www.cambridge.org/9781009618861

DOI: 10.1017/9781009618823

© Benjamin Luke Moorhouse and Kevin M. Wong 2025

This publication is in copyright. Subject to statutory exception and to the provisions of relevant collective licensing agreements, no reproduction of any part may take place without the written permission of Cambridge University Press & Assessment.

When citing this work, please include a reference to the DOI 10.1017/9781009618823

First published 2025

A catalogue record for this publication is available from the British Library

ISBN 978-1-009-61886-1 Hardback
ISBN 978-1-009-61881-6 Paperback
ISSN 2977-3741 (online)
ISSN 2977-3733 (print)

Additional resources for this publication at www.cambridge.org/moorhouse-wong

Cambridge University Press & Assessment has no responsibility for the persistence or accuracy of URLs for external or third-party internet websites referred to in this publication and does not guarantee that any content on such websites is, or will remain, accurate or appropriate.

For EU product safety concerns, contact us at Calle de José Abascal, 56, 1°, 28003 Madrid, Spain, or email eugpsr@cambridge.org

Generative Artificial Intelligence and Language Teaching

Elements in Generative AI in Education

DOI: 10.1017/9781009618823
First published online: June 2025

Benjamin Luke Moorhouse
City University of Hong Kong

Kevin M. Wong
Pepperdine University

Author for correspondence: Benjamin Luke Moorhouse, bmoorhou@cityu.edu.hk

Abstract: The development of generative artificial intelligence (GenAI) has led to intense wonder, surprise, excitement, and concern within the language teaching profession. These tools offer the potential to assist language teachers in helping their learners achieve their language learning goals, and, at the same time, risk disrupting language teaching and learning processes, the teaching profession, and possibly the instrumental needs to learn foreign languages. This Element provides an accessible introduction and guide to the use of GenAI for language teaching. It aims to facilitate language teachers' development of the professional knowledge and skills they need to use GenAI responsibly, ethically, and effectively. It is a valuable resource for pre-service and in-service language teachers of all experience levels. Each section includes helpful tips and questions for reflection to get teachers started with GenAI while ensuring they engage critically and responsibly with these tools. Evidence-informed approaches are promoted throughout the Element.

Keywords: generative AI, language teaching, professional digital competence, evidence-informed, AI literacy

© Benjamin Luke Moorhouse and Kevin M. Wong 2025

ISBNs: 9781009618861 (HB), 9781009618816 (PB), 9781009618823 (OC)
ISSNs: 2977-3741 (online), 2977-3733 (print)

Contents

	Introduction	1
1	Generative AI	3
2	Using GenAI as a Knowledge Resource and Development Tool	15
3	Using GenAI to Assist with Lesson Planning and Materials Preparation	24
4	Using GenAI to Assist with Assessments and Feedback	33
5	Students' Use of GenAI in Language Learning	40
6	Ethical and Social Considerations with GenAI in Language Teaching	51
7	Essential GenAI Skills and Knowledge	60
8	Enhancing Professional GenAI Competence through Professional Development	71
	References	78

An Online Appendix for this Element is available at www.cambridge.org/moorhouse-wong

Introduction*

The public release of ChatGPT by OpenAI in November 2022, and the subsequent release of a plethora of generative artificial intelligence (GenAI) tools by different technology companies, has led to intense wonder, surprise, excitement, concern, and worry about their capabilities (Moorhouse, 2024). These tools offer the potential to assist language teachers in helping their learners achieve their language learning goals, and, at the same time, risk disrupting language teaching and learning processes, the teaching profession, and possibly the instrumental needs to learn foreign languages (Jeon & Lee, 2023; Moorhouse & Kohnke, 2024). We believe that teachers are essential to effective and holistic learning, and they will not be replaced by artificial intelligence (AI), however, AI could help augment their abilities and intelligence. It is important for language teachers to develop the knowledge and skills associated with using GenAI to help their learners navigate the GenAI-infused world but also become critically informed about the ethical and social issues associated with these tools' development. To do this, teachers should model ethical, legal, and safe ways to use GenAI (Hockly, 2023) and help learners think critically about how AI shapes and changes society. At the same time, it is imperative that language teachers can distinguish between the 'hype' surrounding these tools, and evidence-informed professional use of GenAI. This allows language teachers to have greater agency in their use of GenAI tools with thoughtful consideration for how GenAI may shape language teaching. Although language teachers' digital competencies and confidence in using technology have increased since the Covid-19 pandemic, which forced teachers to use technology to mediate teaching and learning (Lee & Jeon, 2024; Moorhouse, 2023), the complex and diverse uses of GenAI tools necessitate unique competencies (Ng et al., 2023).

This Element is centred around the idea that language teachers need new and specific skills and knowledge to use GenAI in their professional practices. We argue that these tools are so different from previous technological advancements that developing these skills and knowledge are essential to the profession (Mishra et al., 2023; Ng et al., 2023). Although there are various frameworks that can be used to help conceptualise the competencies needed to use technology (e.g., technological pedagogical content knowledge), in this Element, we have adapted professional digital competence (Instefjord & Munthe, 2017). Professional digital competence conceptualises that different professions utilise technology differently in their professional practices (Knoth et al., 2024), and, therefore, the knowledge and skills needed to use technology are different. For example, a doctor and a language

---

* Emojis used under a creative commons licence, © X Corp. Full details: Copyright 2025 X Corp and other contributors Code licensed under the MIT Licence: http://opensource.org/licenses/MIT Graphics licensed under CC-BY 4.0: https://creativecommons.org/licenses/by/4.0/.

teacher will use different technologies or even the same technologies in different ways than each other as part of their professional practices. Yet, both need a level of digital competence to effectively engage in their professional tasks and be considered professionally competent (Knoth et al., 2024). Equally, GenAI is affecting each profession differently. A doctor may need to understand and apply the use of AI in medical diagnostic processes. In contrast, a language teacher may need to guide students in how to use GenAI tools to engage in language practice activities. Therefore, in this Element, we adopt five aspects of a newly conceptualised construct, 'professional-GenAI-competence' (P-GenAI-C), to conceptualise the knowledge and skills needed by language teachers in the GenAI world. The aim is that by engaging with this Element, language teachers can develop these five aspects and, therefore, be able to implement GenAI tools effectively and responsibly into their professional practices. The five aspects are:

1. GenAI technological proficiency: Technological proficiency is concerned with teachers' awareness of a variety of GenAI tools, including their functions, uses, and affordances.
2. Pedagogical compatibility of GenAI in English language teaching (PC): PC refers to teachers' use of GenAI tools to supplement and enhance their students' English language learning, including using GenAI tools to help them achieve their learning objectives.
3. Teachers' professional work: Professional work is concerned with the use of GenAI tools in teachers' professional work outside of the classroom, including grading and giving feedback, communicating with stakeholders, and school administration.
4. Risk, well-being, and the ethical use of GenAI (EU): EU refers to teachers' awareness of the risks associated with using AI, the effects that GenAI tools may have on teacher and learner well-being, and the ethical issues pertaining to the use of GenAI tools.
5. Preparation of students for a GenAI world: Preparation of students relates to a teacher's abilities to prepare their students with the knowledge and skills needed to critically and productively engage in GenAI tools in their learning, recreation time, and future work.

Aspects of P-GenAI-C will be referred to throughout the Element, with case studies and questions used to help readers develop their P-GenAI-C.

Element Overview

This Element has eight sections. In Section 1, the question 'What is GenAI?' is addressed along with details of different kinds of GenAI tools and their capabilities. Section 2 explores how GenAI tools can be used to assist teachers as a knowledge resources and development tool. In Section 3, the attention moves to examining how GenAI can assist with lesson planning and materials preparation. Section 4 focuses on the use of GenAI in assisting teachers with assessments and feedback. In Section 5, we consider the roles GenAI can play in supporting students' language learning. Section 6 puts forth important ethical and social issues related to GenAI use in language teaching and learning. In Section 7, essential knowledge and skills language teachers need to effectively engage with GenAI are provided. Finally, Section 8 focuses on the future and how language teachers can stay up to date with relevant developments and continue to evolve their practices to the latest technological advancements in the GenAI age.

The Element provides an accessible introduction and guide to the use of GenAI and language teaching. It is a valuable resource for pre-service and in-service language teachers of all experience levels. Each section includes helpful tips and questions for reflection to get teachers started with GenAI while ensuring they engage critically and responsibly with these tools. Evidence-informed approaches are promoted throughout the Element.

GenAI Use in This Element

Throughout the Element, various GenAI tools are referenced and used to illustrate the capabilities and limitations of the tools for language teaching and learning purposes (see Appendix 1, available online at [short url], for the list of tools referenced in this Element). It is important to note that the tools selected are only a sample of the tools available, and we do not endorse any specific company or product in this Element. Readers can take reference from the Element but are advised to explore the variety of tools available to them and select the most appropriate ones for their context and needs. As the capabilities and features of GenAI tools are constantly advancing, the reader's experience of the tools may be different from the examples provided in the Element. However, we hope the content and skills explored inspire readers to try out these tools in their professional practices.

1 Generative AI

GenAI-Generated Summary of the Section

We thought it would be fun to demonstrate the potential of GenAI in the Element itself. Along with many examples embedded in the sections, we will also provide a GenAI summary of each section in different genres. For Section 1, we asked GPT-4.o for a simple summary. Our prompt was:

This is the first section of a book designed as a resource for language teachers and scholars interested in the application of generative AI tools in language teaching. Can you write a 100-word summary of the section as a lead-in to the section to demonstrate the capabilities you have to provide contextualised summaries of extended texts?

The conversational AI chatbot created the following summary:

> **Summary of Section 1: Generative Artificial Intelligence** This section introduces Generative Artificial Intelligence (GenAI), highlighting its transformative potential in language teaching. It contrasts GenAI tools, such as large language models (LLMs) like ChatGPT, with traditional rule-based AI tools. Unlike earlier AI systems, GenAI leverages deep learning and extensive datasets to generate diverse content, from text and images to audio and video, in response to user prompts. The section categorizes GenAI tools into conversational AI chatbots, visual/audio/video generators, and tools with embedded GenAI functions. It emphasizes their adaptability, speed, and evolving capabilities while raising questions about their impact and ethical considerations in educational contexts.

We can see from the summary that the GenAI tool successfully identified the main points from the section and succinctly and accurately summarised them in a coherent text.

What Is GenAI?

The question, 'What is GenAI?' is not as easy to answer as one might think. First, we should consider the term, artificial intelligence. Generally, AI refers to computer systems that utilise algorithms to mimic human cognitive abilities and carry out tasks traditionally needing human intelligence, such as speech recognition, decision-making, and pattern identification (Ali et al., 2024; Sheikh et al., 2023). It is a broad concept that is used to encapsulate a diverse range of technological functionalities, including robotics, recommendation systems, voice recognition, and chatbots.

In language teaching, before the release of ChatGPT, two types of AI tools were commonly promoted by language educators and scholars for several years due to their perceived utility in assisting language learning – chatbots and digital writing assistants (Fryer et al., 2020; Kohnke, 2023). Chatbots could simulate specific interlocutors (e.g., customer service agents) and discuss particular topics (Kohnke, 2023). They could be used to provide opportunities for language learners to practice specific interactions (Chiu et al., 2023). Digital writing assistants can provide corrective feedback on learners' written work (Lee, 2020), including individualised feedback on students' writing. However, these kinds of AI-powered tools are rule-based programs based on predefined guidelines derived from external knowledge –sometimes called predictive AI. Each tool was designed to perform a specific role and could not deviate from its pre-programmed answers. As such, the functions of technological tools were determined during their programming and inception, limiting the outputs or tasks they could engage in. For example, a chatbot designed to be a customer service agent for a public transportation service could respond to users' queries about the time of the next train but could not respond on other topics or in other roles (unless trained to do so) (Chiu et al., 2023). While researchers saw the potential of these kinds of rule-based AIs in language teaching, due to their narrow functionality, they have experienced very limited uptake in language classrooms. Generative AI is different from these rule-based AI tools. It is easy to see why their arrival has been heralded as a technological revolution that has the potential to transform how we work, play, relate, and learn (Meniado, 2023; Moorhouse et al., 2023).

Generative AI refers to a subset of AI designed for generating various types of content, including text, code, videos, and images (Chan & Colloton, 2024). Among the most popular GenAI tools in language teaching are large language models (LLMs), such as generative pretraining transformers (GPTs), which include OpenAI's ChatGPT and Anthropic's Claude platforms. These LLMs utilise deep learning techniques and extensive datasets sourced from the internet or specialised knowledge bases to produce new and often surprising content in response to diverse and complex prompts like scenarios, images, instructions, or questions (Lim et al., 2023). Instead of relying on predefined rules, LLMs generate content by identifying patterns and relationships within the data to produce statistically probable outcomes (Fui-Hoon Nah et al., 2023). For example, they can predict the next word or token in a sentence to craft coherent text. The adaptability of LLMs like GPTs allows them to be used in various contexts to perform numerous natural language processing tasks without specific instructions (Ali et al., 2024). Extensive training has been used to increase the reliability and predictability of these tools. Moreover, GenAI tools work extremely fast – usually producing content in seconds (Moorhouse, 2024).

Besides LLMs, other models have been developed to analyse and create visual and audio data (e.g., generative adversarial networks (GANs)). Some GenAI tools combine LLMs and GANs to provide an easy-to-use interface using natural language that generates multimodal output. Generative AI tools have incredible functionality. This is why a user can ask an image-generating GenAI tool, such as Dall-E 3, to create an image using natural language, for example, prompting 'an elephant flying a plane with a monkey on its shoulder' and allowing the tool to interpret and create a unique output (see Figure 1 for the hilarious result).

Figure 1 A Dall-E 3-created image of the prompt: An elephant flying a plane with a monkey on its shoulder.

Types of GenAI Tools

It can be challenging to neatly categorise the different kinds of GenAI tools currently available for language teachers. Many tools have multiple functionalities and combine different AI technologies to make them easy to use while performing highly advanced tasks. Some tools are designed for very specific tasks and professions (e.g., medical diagnostic tools) and others are for general application (e.g., conversational AI chatbots). The field is moving incredibly quickly and the types and functionalities of GenAI continue to expand exponentially. One way to classify GenAI tools for language teaching is according to the following three categories: 1. conversational AI chatbots; 2. visual, audio, and video generators; and 3. tools with embedded GenAI functions and specialist AI tools.

Conversational AI Chatbots

Conversational AI chatbots is another name for LLM-based chatbots of GenAI chatbots, with the terms often used interchangeably within language teaching literature. The term 'conversational AI chatbots' predates LLM development and was used to describe rule-based chatbots. It has continued to be used to describe LLM-based chatbots. In this Element, we use conversational AI chatbots to refer to LLM-based AI tools. This category includes models by OpenAI (e.g., ChatGPT 3.0, GPT-4.o), Google (e.g., Gemini 1.5-Flash), Anthropic (e.g., Claude), and Meta (e.g., Llama). These AI tools have a human-like conversational interface where the user can engage with the tool using natural language (e.g., posing questions, giving responses, making statements). All these models can interpret written text input or prompts, with some able to analyse and interpret multi-modal inputs (e.g., texts, images, and videos). Each model has different strengths and limitations (see Section 7 for a more detailed discussion of the differences between AI models). Large language models can be combined with other types of AI architecture (e.g., GANs) to create multi-modal outputs. They can conduct a wide range of human-like tasks. Here are some tasks conversational AI chatbots can perform:

Content Creation

Conversational AI chatbots can generate a broad selection of human-like texts due to the large dataset from which AI tools draw. Users can specify the genre, audience, topic, length, style, and any other desired features, and the tools will generate a relevant text that aligns with the provided specifications. This can include creative works such as specific kinds of poems, songs, and stories; texts for personal and professional communication, such as e-mails, letters, or social media posts; and academic texts, such as argumentative essays, persuasive texts, opinion pieces, and expositions. For example, a primary school language teacher may wish to create a poem on a specific topic or theme they are exploring in their unit, and include some of the key vocabulary from the unit in the poem. They could prompt a conversational AI chatbot with their specifications, and it will generate content following the details in the prompt. For example, the prompt could be, 'Write a three-stanza poem for young language learners in Hong Kong on the topic of transport. Include the following words in the poem: bus, car, taxi, tram, train, bicycle.' A chatbot (e.g., GPT-4.0) would create a poem like this one:

> In Hong Kong's streets, the buses go,
> Through bustling lanes, both high and low.
> With cars and taxis zipping fast,
> We watch the lively city cast.
>
> The trams glide by on tracks so neat,
> A charming way to tour each street.
> The trains beneath the ground, they zoom,
> Through tunnels dark, they pierce the gloom.
>
> On bicycles, we pedal free,
> By parks and shores beside the sea.
> In Hong Kong's transport, near and far,
>
> Adventure waits with each new star.

Teachers can then interact with the conversational AI chatbot to modify the generated content to better meet their needs. For example, the teacher may feel the poem is too challenging for his/her learners. He/she can input a follow-up prompt suggestion to modify the poem for the learners. The prompt could be: 'Can you reduce the lexical demands in the poem?' A chatbot (e.g., GPT-4.o) would create a modified poem like this one:

> Hong Kong Rides
>
> In Hong Kong, buses go,
> Through busy streets, high and low.
> Cars and taxis drive so fast,
> We watch the city as they pass.
>
> Trams on tracks, they glide so slow,
> Through the streets, nice and low.
> Trains zoom fast, under the ground,
> In the tunnels, all around.
>
> On bicycles, we ride with glee,
> By the park and near the sea.
> In Hong Kong, with every ride,
> We find fun and joy inside.

The teacher can continue to interact with the conversational AI chatbot to modify the text (e.g., text difficulty or change the context/topic of the poem), or task it with creating related content (e.g., comprehension questions, other genres or text types using the same topic). The teacher can also end the interactional sequence by 'clearing context' and start a new sequence or conversation.

Conversation Partner

Conversational AI chatbots can engage in coherent contextualised back-and-forth conversations on a multitude of topics and scenarios. This means they can be given a 'role' and can engage in a conversation in that role, including interacting with job interviewers, customers, friends, teachers, or even famous fictional characters. Users can provide a character description of the alias that the conversational AI chatbot is adopting. For example, a disgruntled customer, a supportive colleague, or a demanding job interviewer. Here is an example interaction with GPT-4.o playing the role of a disgruntled customer:

> Initial Prompt: I am a sales assistant in an electronics shop. I want to practice my customer service skills. Can you take up the role of a disgruntled customer who bought a new toaster that they are not satisfied with?

> GPT-4.o: Sure! Let's roleplay. I'll be the disgruntled customer, and you can practice handling the situation. Let's begin: *Customer: Excuse me! I need to speak with someone about this toaster I bought here last week. It's absolutely useless! I can't believe you sell such low-quality products. It doesn't even toast bread properly!*
>
> User: I'm sorry to hear that. Can you describe to me how you use it?
>
> GPT-4.o as customer: *How I use it? I mean, it's a toaster – it's not rocket science! I plug it in, pop the bread in, and press the lever. But no matter what setting I use, it either burns the bread to a crisp or barely warms it up! I shouldn't have to fiddle with it every single time just to get it to work right.*
>
> User: How can a help solve this issue?
>
> GPT-4.o as customer: *Well, for starters, I'd like a toaster that actually works! I paid good money for this one, and it's been nothing but a headache. Are you going to replace it, or do I have to take this up with someone higher up?*

In this interaction, the conversational AI chatbot accurately imitates the language features related to the role as well as the persona it has been asked to adopt. The use of language and phrases such as, 'It's absolutely useless' and 'Well, for starters . . .' show the likely frustrations expected from a disgruntled customer.

Given the large databases that many of the conversational AI chatbots draw from, they are able to imitate the 'spirit' and 'mannerisms' of fictional characters or famous people (although adopting another persona may have ethical implications – see Section 6 for a detailed discussion). Some conversational AI chatbots may remind users that they are not the actual person the user is interacting with before they start the conversation. For example, GPT-4.o was asked to take on the persona of Roald Dahl, the famous children's author, and answer questions about his life:

> Initial prompt: Could you take on the persona of Roald Dahl and answer questions about your life as him with short answers?
>
> GPT-4.o: Of course! I'll take on the persona of Roald Dahl and answer your questions as if I were him. Fire away!
>
> User: Why did you start writing children's books?
>
> GPT-4.o as Roald Dahl: Ah, well, I started writing children's books because I wanted to entertain my own children. I loved telling them bedtime stories, and their laughter and excitement inspired me to write tales that could delight children everywhere. Plus, there's nothing quite like the imagination of a child!
>
> User: Which was the first book you wrote?
>
> GPT-4.o as Roald Dahl: The first children's book I wrote was The Gremlins in 1943. It was inspired by RAF folklore during my time as a pilot. But my first real success in children's literature came later with James and the Giant Peach in 1961. That's when the magic truly began!

As this conversation shows, the conversational AI chatbot can provide accurate information and adopt the language common in the famous person's writings or speeches. Some AI models support oral input and output, allowing for spoken interaction. Of course, GenAI tools can provide inaccurate information (see Section 6 for more details).

(Multi-Modal) Text Evaluation, Summarisation, and Analysis

Most conversational AI chatbot models can read various kinds of multi-modal texts, including written texts, tables, graphics, figures, photos, audio files, and videos. This allows them to conduct a multitude of operations, including describing, evaluating, summarising, categorising, and analysing the inputted content.

For written texts, such as creative works, articles, or books, conversational AI chatbots can be tasked with summarising, analysing, or providing suggestions on how to modify, adapt, or improve the texts. For example, a user could input an article and ask for a summary of the text or create a social media post promoting the text. Figure 2 shows how an AI (GPT-4.o) was able to read the content of the article, extract key information, and create a coherent and accurate LinkedIn post in the style of promotional social media posts. The initial prompt was, 'Can you create a LinkedIn post promoting this article. Keep it short. Use emojis to attract the reader. [Article attached].'

Users can provide specific instructions to the conversational AI chatbot on how to treat the inputted text, such as providing rubrics. In addition, a user could

How has the pandemic reshaped teaching?

Check out this fascinating article by Benjamin Luke Moorhouse on how **primary-school English-language teachers** integrated **digital technologies** into their classrooms after online teaching during COVID-19.

Key insights include:
- Greater use of **Learning Management Systems**
- Embracing **interactive digital tools** like quizzes & presentations
- Creative use of **digital noticeboards**
- Lessons on balancing tech use with traditional methods

This study highlights how challenges can spark **innovation** in education. A must-read for educators navigating the digital age!

🔗 Read the full article here

#EdTech #ELT #DigitalTeaching #EducationInnovation #TeacherDevelopmen

Figure 2 An example of a user inputting a text, and the conversational AI chatbot creating a LinkedIn post to promote the text.

input a story and evaluate its lexical complexity, suggest ways to improve the writing quality, or increase its originality.

For multi-modal content (recorded and live), some of these tools can understand content and infer information about the content (e.g., where the photo was taken). Figure 3 shows a photograph taken by Benjamin Luke Moorhouse in a supermarket in Hong Kong.

The photograph was uploaded to GPT-4.5-preview with the prompt, 'Where was this photograph taken?' The conversational AI chatbot was able to interpret the photograph. The chatbot generated the following text:

> This photo was likely taken in Hong Kong. This conclusion is based on the presence of "Kowloon Dairy," a well-known dairy brand in Hong Kong, the pricing labels using the "$" symbol (HKD is represented by "$"), and the presence of Chinese and English text, which is typical in Hong Kong supermarkets.

The tool correctly identifies the content and uses the language of the texts in the image to infer that it was taken in Hong Kong. It can identify physical characteristics, emotions, and gestures. A photo of Benjamin Luke Moorhouse was uploaded to GPT-4.5 (Figure 4).

The chatbot was asked to describe the person in the photo. The chatbot created the following description:

> The person in the photo appears to be sitting indoors, with a bright background provided by large windows. They have short brown hair and are wearing a dark-colored shirt with white stripes. They are smiling and appear cheerful.

Figure 3 Photo inputted into a conversational AI chatbot (taken by Benjamin Luke Moorhouse).

Figure 4 Photo inputted into a conversational AI chatbot (taken by Benjamin Luke Moorhouse).

The example shows how a conversational AI chatbot can correctly describe the physical appearance of a person and identify their emotions. Some of the latest GenAI models can use a mobile phone's built-in camera to provide live, real-time descriptions of the physical environment around the user.

Translation and Interpretation

Conversational AI chatbots can translate and interpret texts quite accurately, often outperforming previous specialist translation tools. This may be related to their ability to interpret context in the texts they are tasked with translating, which can be enhanced when the user provides contextual information in their prompts. Importantly, the accuracy of the translation will depend on the languages being translated. There are specialist translation tools that utilise GenAI models and architecture to provide more accurate and reliable translations (e.g., DeepL). Some tools can translate oral texts and produce oral texts. Figure 5 shows how a chatbot translated the LinkedIn post in Figure 2 into two languages suggested by the user. We used the prompt: 'Can you translate the post into French and Japanese?'

A defining feature of conversational AI chatbots is their ability to 'remember' and 'recall' previous prompts and maintain coherent and contextualised interactional sequences. This means teachers can engage in an iterative process of prompting and refinement until the desired content is produced. See Section 7 for more detailed descriptions of the ways chatbots work.

> **French Translation**
> 🌐 **Comment la pandémie a-t-elle transformé l'enseignement ?**
> Découvrez cet article fascinant de Benjamin Luke Moorhouse sur la manière dont les **enseignants d'anglais en école primaire** ont intégré les **technologies numériques** dans leurs classes après avoir enseigné en ligne pendant la pandémie de COVID-19.
> Points clés :
> ☑ Utilisation accrue des **systèmes de gestion de l'apprentissage**
> ☑ Adoption d'outils numériques interactifs comme des **quiz et présentations**
> ☑ Utilisation créative des **tableaux d'affichage numériques**
> ☑ Réflexion sur l'équilibre entre technologie et méthodes traditionnelles
> Cette étude montre comment les défis peuvent stimuler l'**innovation** dans l'éducation. Un article incontournable pour les enseignants à l'ère numérique ! 🌐📚
> 🔗 Lisez l'article complet ici
> #EdTech #ELT #EnseignementNumérique #InnovationÉducative #DéveloppementEnseignant
>
> **Japanese Translation**
> 🌐 パンデミックが教育をどう変えたか？
> COVID-19パンデミック中のオンライン授業を経て、小学校の英語教師がどのようにして教室にデジタル技術を取り入れたのか、Benjamin Luke Moorhouse氏の興味深い記事をご紹介します。
> 注目ポイント：
> ☑ 学習管理システムの利用拡大
> ☑ クイズやプレゼンテーションなどのインタラクティブなデジタルツールの採用
> ☑ デジタル掲示板の創造的な活用
> ☑ テクノロジーと伝統的な方法のバランスを考える重要性
> この研究は、困難がどのようにして教育におけるイノベーションを促進するかを示しています。デジタル時代の教育者に必読の一冊です！ 🌐📚
> 🔗 記事を読む
> #EdTech #ELT #デジタル教育 #教育イノベーション #教師の成長

Figure 5 AI-generated translations of the LinkedIn post in Figure 2.

Visual, Audio, and Video Generators

Visual, audio, and video generators can generate specific kinds of content in response to prompts. Usually, the interface is built on an LLM. The user can input their request using natural language, then the tool converts the request into language (and adds additional information programmed by the technology company), which the user cannot see, before producing the output. Some of these tools create 'one-off' images that the user cannot modify directly in the tool, while others allow the user to modify and adapt the image using follow-up prompts. Some specialist image editing tools allow users to work directly with the image to modify and change specific parts of it. Common visual generators include Dall-E, Stable Diffusion, and MidJourney. Specialist tools include Adobe Firefly.

Audio generators can create audio output from written or audio input. Some are specifically designed to create music (e.g., Jukebox), while others can produce natural-sounding speech in different accents and speaking styles (e.g., Speechflow AI). Tools such as Heygen allow users to input text in one language, and have it translated and produced orally in another. Users can select an avatar to present the speech, or impose the audio on an original video. Most recently, video-generation tools, such as Sora AI, have entered the GenAI landscape, which can generate short video clips from written prompts. Given their ability to interpret natural language prompts, they can create highly creative video clips, as well as life-like scenes. They have also allowed for the creation of interactive avatars that people can interact with in real-time.

Tools with Embedded GenAI Functions and Specialist AI Tools

Given the capabilities of GenAI models, many existing digital tools are embedding GenAI functions and features into their tools to increase automation and enhance productivity, ultimately speeding up task completion (Moorhouse, 2024). It is likely this trend will continue as users benefit from automating specific aspects of their tasks, commonly known as 'AI assistants' or 'AI co-pilots'. For example, the Quiz platform Kahoot! has a built-in AI assistance feature that can help users generate quiz questions. As another example, the student response system Mentimeter has an AI function that automatically organises open responses submitted by individuals.

There are also specialist AI tools that have been developed for specific uses or communities. For example, MagicSchool.ai is an AI tool designed for schools and teachers that has features that can automate common teaching-related tasks. Teachers can input their requirements and contextual information and generate tailored content as output. Tools include rubric generators, lesson plan generators, text levellers, YouTube summarisers, e-mail writers, and many more. It is likely that AI assistants will be embedded in increasingly more digital tools, and new tools will be developed to meet certain community needs.

Conclusion

This section introduced the definition and characteristics of GenAI tools and the different kinds of GenAI tools that language teachers might use. This knowledge is an important aspect of P-GenAI-C. Knowing how the tools work and the different kinds of tools available allows teachers to select appropriate tools for their professional tasks. The field of GenAI is moving incredibly fast and even at the point of writing this Element, new tools and new features of existing tools have been developed and released. In subsequent sections, other aspects of P-GenAI-C will be addressed.

Questions for Reflection

1. What capabilities of GenAI tools do you think will help you most with your language teaching?
2. Which GenAI tools are you most excited to try out in your language teaching?
3. What concerns do you have about the impact of these tools on language teaching, learning, or beyond?

2 Using GenAI as a Knowledge Resource and Development Tool

GenAI-Generated Summary of the Section

In this section, we asked GPT-4.o to summarise the section as a poem. This shows how conversational AI chatbots can interpret the context of an uploaded text and create a coherent and somewhat creative genre. This is the poem it generated:

The Teacher's AI Companion
In classrooms vast, both near and far,
Where lessons live and learners spar,
No single method holds the key,
To teach with grace and mastery.

From rods of color to silent ways,
To themes of life and future days,
GenAI steps to lend its might,
A guiding hand, a spark of light.

It draws from worlds both old and new,
With knowledge vast, perspectives true,
Yet caution calls – its flaws may hide,
So verify, and check each side.

For cultures rich and tongues diverse,
It helps us bridge, connect, immerse,
To learn the needs of every face,
And build a warm, inclusive space.

> Through prompts we craft, it helps us see,
> The ways to teach creatively,
> With feedback sharp, and plans in hand,
> We navigate this teaching land.
>
> So teachers rise, embrace the aid,
> Of GenAI tools carefully made,
> For though the path is yours to chart,
> It offers wisdom, a helping heart.

Key aspects of a poem are clearly evident in the generated text, and anyone can recognise this as a poem. The poem content aligns with the section's themes. There is evidence of creative language use, including rhyme (e.g., far and spar), imagery, (e.g., a guiding hand, a spark of light), personification (e.g., It offers wisdom, a helping heart) and alliteration (e.g., lessons live and learners spar). The question of whether GenAI tools can actually be creative is debatable. However, a study found that people prefer GenAI-generated poems to human-written poems (see Porter & Machery, 2024).

Introduction

In Section 1, the capabilities of GenAI tools were introduced. These immense capabilities have led to intense interest in the language teaching community about how they can assist with language teaching and learning. This section builds on Section 1 by exploring effective uses of GenAI tools in language teaching and focuses on developing language teachers' PC, which is an aspect of P-GenAI-C. To do this, we need to first consider what constitutes language teaching and the wonderfully diverse world that language teachers can find themselves teaching in.

Before we begin exploring the pedagogical uses of GenAI in language teaching, it is important to remember that language teachers can find themselves in a variety of diverse teaching contexts and modalities. Language teaching happens at all levels of formal education (nursery, primary, secondary, tertiary, and beyond). Class sizes can vary from one-on-one settings to classrooms with hundreds of learners. Teachers can conduct language lessons that are synchronously online, face-to-face, or hybrid (a combination of face-to-face and synchronous online). Teachers can teach through only one mode, blending online and face-to-face modes, or straddle asynchronous and synchronous online modes in a teaching sequence. Teachers might even find themselves teaching in immersive virtual reality (VR) environments, such as the metaverse.

Language teachers can have a pre-set curriculum with assigned teaching materials and standardised assessment tasks or be given full autonomy and responsibility to develop their own curriculum, instruction, and assessments. They can teach in programmes or courses that have specific learning objectives and focuses (e.g., International English Language Testing System (IELTS) preparation courses, English in the disciplines, or English for Academic Purposes), or they can teach general language courses. Lessons can occur daily, weekly, or occasionally. Classes can also be streamed by proficiency or be mixed by ability and proficiency. Students' readiness, interest, and learning profiles (e.g., background, culture, or language resources (including first languages [L1s])) can differ between and in learning contexts and classes (Tomlinson, 2014). The diversity of language teaching and learning contexts and modalities is almost endless.

Similarly, there is no 'one-size-fits-all' method or approach that language teachers can adopt to guarantee success in any or all contexts (Richards & Rogers, 2014). We do know, from years of research, that there are certain evidence-based principles to effective language teaching that can be applied to most contexts, such as, clearly establishing learning goals, comprehensible exposure to the target language, meaningful communication, authentic materials, regular and varied practice, timely and constructive feedback, differentiated instruction, cultivating positive and supportive classroom environments, regular formative assessment and monitoring, and reflective practice (Richards, 2010). However, despite the multitudes of books, articles, videos, organisations, online resources, teacher training, and professional development that are available to assist language teachers, they can still struggle to develop effective learning environments and help their learners achieve their language learning goals. In addition, language teaching can be cognitively, emotionally, and physically intense with teachers engaged in a plethora of (often simultaneous) tasks, such as sourcing and creating materials, designing relevant teaching plans and materials, catering for learner diversity, managing classroom behaviour, and assessing and providing feedback on learning.

In this and subsequent sections, we argue that GenAI has the potential to assist teachers in implementing evidence-based language teaching principles within the diverse teaching contexts and modalities they may be teaching in.

Knowledge Resource and Development

The capabilities of GenAI, specifically conversational AI chatbots, that draw on vast datasets and produce contextually relevant responses, means they have potential in acting as a knowledge resource and developer for language teachers (Moorhouse, 2024). Conversational AI chatbots can provide accurate information on a range of topics, teaching methodologies and approaches, languages, cultures, and societies.

Using GenAI to Support Teachers' Topic and Content Knowledge Development

In terms of topic and content, when well-prompted, chatbots can generate detailed information about science, medicine, famous people, history, places, and almost any natural, physical or social phenomenon within a specific date range (Kasneci et al., 2023; Wang et al., 2024). Although not content specialists, language teachers are often expected to have knowledge about various topics and themes to support students' content and academic learning, or to implement thematic and task-based teaching approaches. Language teachers can use conversational AI chatbots to seek information and build their topic and content knowledge. For example, a teacher of young language learners who adopts a theme-based approach, organising learning activities around the theme to make cognitive connections for language learning (Pinter, 2017), could prompt a conversational AI (e.g., ChatGPT) to generate information about the theme. For example, a language teacher of young learners might be exploring the theme of 'festivals' with their class. They could prompt a chatbot to give some ideas of interesting festivals. We used GPT-4.o and the prompt: 'Could you provide some information about three European festivals that could be interesting to young English language learners?' It generated accurate information about three festivals: La Tomatina (Spain), Oktoberfest (Germany), and the Carnival of Venice (Italy). Here is an example of the information provided for La Tomatina (Spain):

1. La Tomatina (Spain)
- **What is it?** La Tomatina is a famous tomato-throwing festival held in Buñol, Spain. Participants gather in the streets to throw ripe tomatoes at each other in a fun and messy food fight.
- **When does it happen?** The last Wednesday of August every year.
- **Why is it interesting?** It's a playful and unique tradition that sparks curiosity and laughter among young learners. They can learn English phrases related to food, colors, and actions like *throw*, *splash*, and *squash*.
- **Fun fact:** Over 100 tons of tomatoes are used each year during the event.

Using chatbots in this way can inform and provide inspiration for developing teaching content that teachers can include in their lessons. Teachers should be mindful that these tools can hallucinate and create incorrect information (see Section 6 for more details about GenAI hallucinations and accuracy issues).

Using GenAI to Help Teachers Gain an Understanding of Language Teaching Methodologies and Approaches

There are a plethora of teaching methods and approaches that language teachers can reference when designing curriculum and implementing instruction. Richards and Rodgers (2014) detail 15 approaches and methods in their book *Approaches and Methods in Language Teaching (Third Edition)*, which include task-based language teaching, total physical response, The Silent Way, content-based instruction, and content and language integrated learning, and so on. Although language teachers may be familiar with some of these approaches, they may wish to understand the types of approaches that are best suited to their context or want to learn more about a specific approach with which they are less familiar. Language teachers can prompt a conversational AI chatbot to generate a list of methods and approaches, provide key information about a specific approach, or create example activities and lesson plans that illustrate the implementation of the approach in a specific context. See Appendix 2 (available online at [short url]) for an example of how a language teacher can prompt a conversational AI chatbot to generate a sample lesson plan for a specific teaching method (e.g., The Silent Way developed by Calen Gattegno). The plan provides an accurate illustration of the principles that underpin The Silent Way (e.g., minimum teacher talk) and the learning activities common to this method (e.g., use of Cuisenaire rods to elicit learner responses). The ability of tools to provide contextually relevant lessons and activity examples that adhere to specific teaching methods and approaches can assist teachers in learning and selecting the approaches that align best with their teaching needs (Kohnke et al., 2023).

Using GenAI to Build Awareness of Languages, Cultures, and Societies

Language teachers can work in a variety of diverse contexts with learners from different cultures, societies, and languages. In order to create a supportive and inclusive learning environment, it is important for teachers to develop intercultural and interlanguage awareness (Baker, 2012). When interacting with students and/or their parents or caregivers, knowledge of cultures and languages can help build relationships and rapport (Scarino, 2009). Knowledge of the learners' language repertoires can also help language teachers tailor their curriculum and instruction to common challenges faced by speakers of those language groups. However, it is unlikely that language teachers will have extensive knowledge of the diverse cultures and languages in their classrooms. Teachers can use conversational AI chatbots to conduct research into cultures and languages. This can be particularly useful before a new teaching unit or when designing a curriculum. For example, a secondary school language teacher may be planning to teach a grammar lesson on the use of personal pronouns. In their class, they have speakers of Spanish,

Mandarin, and Japanese. They could ask a conversational AI chatbot to provide a table presenting the personal pronouns in each language, examples of where they can be placed in sentences, and indicate any challenges for Spanish, Mandarin, and Japanese learners of English. Here is an example prompt:

- I am a secondary school language teacher planning to teach a grammar lesson on the use of personal pronouns. In my class, they have speakers of Spanish, Chinese, and Japanese. Provide a table presenting the personal pronouns in each language, examples of where they can be placed in sentences, and indicate any challenges for Spanish, Chinese and Japanese learners of English.

Table 1 shows the kind of response a chatbot can generate.

In this way, the teacher can develop a more targeted lesson that addresses potential learning challenges. Language teachers should know that the tools may provide biased or stereotypical responses, and given the data used to train the AI, and as the majority of the training data for LLMs is in English (93%) compared to 7% for other languages (Brown et al., 2020), the quality and accuracy of the information provided may depend on the amount of data on the language as well as the quality of the prompt provided (Cain, 2023).

Conclusion

As stated at the beginning of this section, language teaching is incredibly diverse. Therefore, it is unreasonable to expect teachers to have all the knowledge they need, or to have access to appropriate and plentiful materials to use with their learners. This section has shown how GenAI tools can assist language teachers in developing the knowledge they need, as well as planning and preparing materials for their lessons. As we conclude this section, we hope readers will feel they have begun to develop an awareness of the pedagogical compatibility of GenAI with language teaching (one aspect of P-GenAI-C). The next section will continue to explore ways language teachers can effectively use GenAI in language teaching, specifically addressing ways in which it can support lesson planning and material development.

Questions for Reflection

1. How might you use GenAI tools to support your knowledge development?
2. What kinds of culture and language diversity do you have in your class, and how could GenAI tools help you learn more about your learners' backgrounds and needs?
3. How do you plan to double check the content created by GenAI tools to ensure the information is reliable?

Table 1 A table generated by GPT-4.o with information about pronouns in three different languages

English pronoun	Spanish	Chinese (Mandarin)	Japanese	Placement examples in English	Challenges for learners
I	Yo	我 (wǒ)	私 (わたし, watashi)	I eat lunch.	**Spanish**: May omit "yo" in Spanish, so students might skip pronouns in English. **Chinese**: No verb conjugation in Chinese; difficulty with "am" in "I am". **Japanese**: Pronouns often omitted in Japanese; students may omit "I".
You (singular)	Tú/Usted	你 (nǐ) / 您 (nín)	あなた (anata)	You are kind.	**Spanish**: Tú/Usted distinction for familiarity/formality, but English lacks this. **Chinese**: Politeness distinction (你 vs. 您). **Japanese**: Rarely use "anata"; might overuse it in English.
He	Él	他 (tā)	彼 (かれ, kare)	He runs fast.	**Spanish**: Gender agreement (él vs. ella); possible confusion with "it". **Chinese**: 他 is pronounced the same as 她 (she), so students may mix up "he" and "she". **Japanese**: Pronouns like "kare" are rarely used; students may omit "he".

Table 1 (cont.)

English pronoun	Spanish	Chinese (Mandarin)	Japanese	Placement examples in English	Challenges for learners
She	Ella	她 (tā)	彼女 (かのじょ, kanojo)	She sings beautifully.	**Spanish**: Gender agreement issues; may confuse "she" and "it". **Chinese**: 他 and 她 sound identical, leading to confusion. **Japanese**: "Kanojo" is rarely used outside specific contexts, leading to omission of "she".
It	(No equivalent)	它 (tā)	(No equivalent)	It is raining.	**Spanish**: No direct equivalent of "it"; may omit subject in English. **Chinese**: 它 is used for objects, but may not be intuitive. **Japanese**: No equivalent for "it"; may omit subject entirely.
We	Nosotros/ Nosotras	我们 (wǒmen)	私たち (わたしたち, watashitachi)	We like pizza.	**Spanish**: Gendered forms (nosotros/ nosotras) may confuse learners. **Chinese**: No gender distinction; may overgeneralize this in English. **Japanese**: Rarely used explicitly in Japanese; may omit "we".

You (plural)	Vosotros/Ustedes	你们 (nǐmen)	あなたたち (anatatachi)	You all are amazing.	**Spanish**: Vosotros is regional; Ustedes is formal, but English lacks this distinction. **Chinese**: Plural marker "们" may not feel natural in English. **Japanese**: Pronoun is rarely used; may overuse "you all".
They	Ellos/Ellas	他们 (tāmen) / 她们 (tāmen)	彼ら (かれら, karera)/彼女たち (かのじょたち, kanojotachi)	They are coming.	**Spanish**: Gender agreement (ellos/ellas); may confuse "they" with "it". **Chinese**: Gender distinction in writing (他们 vs. 她们) but not in pronunciation, leading to confusion. **Japanese**: Rarely use "they"; may omit pronoun entirely.

3 Using GenAI to Assist with Lesson Planning and Materials Preparation

GenAI-Generated Summary of the Section

In this section, we used GPT-4.o to create a short dialogue between two English language teachers discussing the section content:

Dialogue: Two English Language Teachers Discussing Section 3

Teacher A: Have you read Section 3 of the book on using GenAI in language teaching?

Teacher B: Yes, it's fascinating! The idea of using GenAI for lesson planning and materials preparation could save so much time.

Teacher A: Absolutely. I liked how it framed GenAI as a "planning partner." Brainstorming lesson ideas with AI and refining them sounds like having a colleague on call.

Teacher B: Exactly. And the materials preparation section was insightful too. Using AI to generate texts, images, and even differentiated resources tailored to students' levels is a game-changer.

Teacher A: I agree. The practical examples, like paraphrasing activities or creating genre-specific texts, were really helpful. The advice to align materials with evidence-based principles stood out to me.

Teacher B: Same here. I also liked the part about students using AI to create materials. It's a great way to foster engagement and creativity.

Teacher A: True. But we'd still need to refine and adapt what AI generates. The section made it clear that teachers remain central to the process.

Teacher B: Definitely. GenAI is a tool, not a replacement for us. But it's exciting to think about the possibilities it opens up.

Teacher A: Couldn't agree more! Let's try incorporating some of these ideas into our lessons.

Teacher B: Let's do it!

This dialogue shows how the conversational AI chatbot could identify the main themes but present them within a professional conversation with identifiable features of such a conversation. The dialogue appears to be semi-formal, combining both professional vocabulary (e.g., 'evidence-based principles') and conversational elements (e.g., 'It's fascinating'). The interactional structure shows coherency with each speaker 'collaborating' to build on each other's ideas and expressing agreement. However, it is very polished and perhaps reads more like a textbook-style scripted interaction than a real conversation between two colleagues. Changing an academic text to a conversational genre could help teachers and students connect with the content more easily. The script could be inputted into a voice simulator and played back to students. Some GenAI tools can automatically make podcasts of articles to help the listener connect with the content in a more relaxed and conversational style (e.g., Google NotebookLM; Yeo et al., 2025).

Introduction

Studies show that lesson planning is crucial for making the teaching–learning encounter valuable and productive (Rifkin, 2003). It is during planning that teachers can make key decisions about the lesson objectives, content, learning activities, engagement, timing, assessments, and groupings (Richards, 2015). The process of lesson planning helps teachers anticipate potential challenges while identifying clear learning outcomes, leading to better utilisation of lesson time (Scrivener, 2011). Yet, language teachers can struggle to find sufficient time for planning and preparation (Bauml, 2014; König et al., 2020). In addition, scholars suggest that the complexity of language education, with its multiple components such as grammar, vocabulary, pronunciation, and cultural nuances, makes lesson planning particularly daunting for language teachers (Scrivener, 2011).

There has been intense speculation about the utility of GenAI tools in assisting language teachers with their planning and preparation (Bonner et al., 2023; Crompton & Burke 2024; Hong, 2023; Kohnke & Zou, 2024). Bonner et al. (2023) suggested that chatbots have the potential to leverage their extensive knowledge of various educational subjects to help create new lesson ideas across diverse topics. They compared using GenAI in this manner to brainstorming sessions with other educators. The teacher and GenAI can 'discuss' their ideas and evaluate how their plans might benefit and apply to students. Van den Berg and du Plessis (2023) noted that chatbots can effectively generate materials such as lesson plans, visual aids, worksheets, and assessments.

In this section, suggestions on how GenAI can assist teachers with two fundamental yet challenging tasks – lesson planning and materials preparation – are explored, contributing to the knowledge needed for teachers to enhance their students' language learning with the assistance of GenAI.

GenAI-Assisted Lesson Planning

GenAI as a Planning Partner

Language teachers can adopt Bonner et al.'s (2023) ideas and use conversational AI chatbots as simulated colleagues or critical friends in their lesson-planning process. They could ask for lesson sequencing and/or activity ideas based on their planned objectives, teaching points, or needs of learners. Teachers can share their initial lesson plan drafts with a chatbot with the tool asked to evaluate it, propose alternatives, or suggest pre-lesson or post-lesson tasks. At a simple level, the teacher can ask the AI to give activity ideas. For example, an English-for-academic-purposes teacher could prompt the conversational AI chatbot to give activity ideas for helping learners practice the skill of paraphrasing. The teacher can then further prompt to get more ideas, or get more details about one of the suggested ideas. This could stimulate their thinking and provide them with ideas they may not have thought of independently themselves (Crompton & Burke, 2024; Kohnke et al., 2023).

GenAI as a Lesson Plan Creator

At a more complex level, language teachers can work with a conversational AI chatbot to develop a complete lesson sequence or plan. It is important that when prompting the chatbot, the prompt is detailed and provides enough information for it to give useful suggestions (Cain, 2023; Moorhouse et al., 2025). For example, when writing the prompt, language teachers can provide information about the learners (e.g., age, language proficiency, needs), language skills (e.g., writing, reading, speaking, listening), focus (e.g., grammar item, vocabulary list), teaching methods or approaches (e.g., task-based language teaching, presentation-practice-production), number of lessons and lesson lengths, and any other information that would help the AI to generate a more accurate response. Teachers can input a corpus of documents (e.g., curriculum documents, teaching materials) relevant to a course they are building (Kasneci et al., 2023). When given a large task, like creating a lesson sequence or plan, it is likely that the teacher will need to 'work with' the AI in an iterative process until the desired plan is created. This means asking follow-up prompts that help the LLM to finetune the response (Moorhouse et al., 2025) (see Section 7 for prompting techniques).

It is important to remember that when tasking conversational AI chatbots with assisting in lesson plan design, the GenAI tool will not have the deep knowledge of the learners or context that the teacher possesses (van den Berg & du Plessis, 2023). In addition, as the database mirrors human knowledge, suggestions may be inappropriate, biased, generic, or repetitive. We have observed that when tasked with suggesting lesson ideas for young language learners, some of the suggestions are not age-appropriate and would be more effective with older learners. Educators should use GenAI tools as resources and catalysts, and should make the final decision on anything used with their learners (Lee & Jeon, 2024). Teachers are crucial for evaluating, refining, adapting, and implementing lesson plans and materials generated to ensure effective teaching (van den Berg & du Plessis, 2023).

Using GenAI Tools to Assist with Material Preparation

The generative capabilities of GenAI tools mean language teachers can make almost any kind of multimodal material needed to aid instruction. As Section 1 showed, GenAI tools can create various kinds of texts, images, videos, and audio files. It is well understood that language teachers are often dependent on material writers (e.g., textbooks) and may not feel confident to develop their own materials (McGrath, 2016). Yet, selecting, evaluating, adapting, or creating materials to the local context and learners' needs can increase their relevance and usefulness in the learning process (Tomlinson, 2015). By seeing GenAI tools as teaching assistants with the capability of generating tailored content (Moorhouse, 2024), language teachers can better align their materials with learner readiness, interests, needs, and profiles.

Tomlinson (2015) summarises five universal principles for materials development and evaluation:

1) exposure to the language in use,
2) affective engagement,
3) cognitive engagement,
4) meaning-related attention to form, and
5) opportunity for language for communication.

Teachers can work with GenAI tools to select, evaluate, adapt, or create materials that align with these principles, local considerations, and contextual needs. Research demonstrates that to design materials that expose learners to language in use, the materials should be comprehensible, meaningful, authentic, substantial in quality and valuable in variety, and provide opportunities for language experiences in a variety of ways (McGrath, 2016). It can be hard for commercial textbooks to meet all these criteria for diverse learners (McGrath, 2016), which offers an entryway for GenAI tools. Language teachers can work with a conversational AI chatbot to create texts that illustrate the meaning of specific words, or provide examples of specific grammatical structures within an appropriate genre. A language teacher could prompt a conversational AI to generate a specific genre (e.g., recount) that includes a specific context (e.g., theme park in Japan), and a list of words to include (e.g., thrilling, exciting, amazing, boring, exhausting). We used the prompt "Create a recount about a trip to a theme park in Japan that includes the following adjectives: thrilling, exciting, amazing, boring, exhausting. Make sure the context helps the reader interpret the meaning of the adjectives" to prompt GPT-4.o to generate a coherent recount with embedded vocabulary items:

> **My Adventure at the Theme Park in Japan**
> Last summer, I had the opportunity to visit one of the most **thrilling** theme parks in Japan. From the moment we entered, the atmosphere was electric with excitement. The towering roller coasters and intricate designs of the attractions promised an **exciting** day ahead.
> Our first stop was the infamous Dragon's Fury roller coaster. The ride was everything I had hoped for and more. The twists, turns, and loops were absolutely **amazing**. As we hurtled through the air, I could feel my heart racing with exhilaration. The view from the top was breathtaking, offering a panoramic glimpse of the entire park.
> After the roller coaster, we decided to try out a few of the other rides. Unfortunately, the Ferris wheel, which I had high hopes for, turned out to be quite **boring**. It moved at a snail's pace and offered little more than a slow, uneventful circle. However, it did give us a chance to catch our breath and plan our next adventure.
> By mid-afternoon, we had explored nearly every corner of the park, from the haunted houses to the water rides. It was an **exhausting** experience, but in the best possible way. Our legs ached from all the walking, and our faces hurt from smiling so much.
> In the end, our day at the theme park was a perfect blend of **thrilling** rides, **exciting** moments, and the occasional **boring** interlude. Despite the **exhausting** nature of the trip, the memories we made were truly **amazing** and will stay with me forever.

To increase the value of the text for vocabulary exposure, the teacher could prompt the chatbot to ensure the context helps the reader interpret the meaning of the adjectives. This generated text offers contextual clues to support the meaning of target vocabulary words. Although the text could be considered complex, the teacher could work with the tool to simplify it (e.g., "Please adjust the Lexile level."). GenAI tools can create differentiated texts for learners of different language proficiencies and interests or provide multiple texts that expose students to the language a number of times. This could include reducing the lexical demands in a text or creating multiple texts on the same topic at different levels of complexity (Moorhouse, 2024).

Teachers could use conversational AI chats to create a listening script, and then use audio generators, or video generators, to make the texts multimodal. This allows teachers to make listening and viewing materials that can help expose students to a wider range of multimodal texts. Audio and video generators with voice simulation features allow users to select specific accents with increasing exposure. However, most tools are dominated by privileged language varieties and accents (specifically North American) – leading to the risk of increased language variety standardisation. In addition, teachers can prompt chatbots to generate comprehension questions that support learners to read for meaning or develop specific language skills (e.g., inferring). Here is an example of a comprehension question about the previous recount text generated on GPT-4.o:

> What does the word "thrilling" in the context of the theme park describe?
> - A. The slow pace of the Ferris wheel
> - B. The overall atmosphere and roller coasters
> - C. The boring parts of the day
> - D. The exhausting nature of walking around the park

One important consideration when using GenAI to create texts is authenticity. Authenticity is a complex concept and its importance is highly debated in language teaching. At a basic level, authenticity refers to texts created for real-world purposes and not language teaching. However, at a more complex level, the way we engage with the text (e.g., the task) and the learning environment are also important (McGrath, 2016). GenAI makes the concept of 'authenticity' confusing as it blurs the lines of authorship. Yet, the GenAI user is still ultimately the one responsible for the output and will engage the tool with a specific purpose in mind. Whether content created by GenAI tools is authentic or not depends on the purpose for engaging with AI in text generation (e.g., language learning or real-world purpose), what task it is used for (e.g., language practice or communicative task), and the environment the text is situated in. Language teachers should be mindful of the kinds of language that appear in the text they generate with GenAI tools so as to help learners' notice the relationship between language, genre, and context. Given the ease of generating texts using chatbots, GenAI-generated texts could become the primary material used in class and students' main exposure to the target language. However, teachers should not fully rely on AI-generated texts and still integrate books, websites, and human-created texts into their language teaching, given the known benefits they bring to language learning.

Using GenAI to Create Affectively and Cognitively Engaging Materials

Creating learning opportunities that facilitate affective engagement, or emotional responses, can support language learning. GenAI tools can create a wide variety of engaging genres (e.g., jokes, cartoons, songs, stories, poems, games) to engage students. Teachers can prompt the tools to include their students as characters within the literary texts, or could include localised details in their prompts to get contextualise texts to learners' lived experiences and environments. Teachers could use an image generator to create visuals to support the meaning of the text or any specific vocabulary in the text.

Designing materials that require learners to think, or engage cognitively, is essential in second-language (L2) acquisition (Mishan, 2015). To do this, language teachers can design decision-making activities that require students to engage meaningfully with language. For example, when teaching new vocabulary words, learners can be asked to rank, sort, organise, identify, or classify words based on certain criteria, such as personal preferences (likes, dislikes), characteristics, or relationships. Conversational AI chatbots can simplify the process of constructing these kinds of materials. Here are some vocabulary decision-making activities suggested by GPT-4.o for the following word list: swimming, running, singing, dancing, playing football, playing chess, playing badminton, rock climbing, and skiing:

- **Activity 1: Categorisation:** Categorise the activities into the following groups: *Outdoor Activities, Indoor Activities, Solo Activities,* and *Team Activities.*
- **Activity 2: Matching:** Match each activity with the appropriate equipment or setting (e.g., swimming ➔ swimming pool)
- **Activity 3: Ranking Exercise:** Rank the activities from most to least enjoyable based on your personal preferences. Share your ranking with a partner and explain your choices.

Using GenAI to Create Form Focused Materials

Explicit attention to language form is an important aspect of language learning as language learners notice and practice language (Thornbury, 1999). Conversational AI chatbots can assist teachers in creating a variety of materials that help learners strengthen the form/meaning relationship. Chatbots can create worksheets that focus on specific grammar items, vocabulary items, reading, or other skills. For example, a secondary school English language teacher could be teaching students to practise the appropriateness of the passive and active voices depending on their communicative function. A chatbot could be tasked with providing practice ideas and creating a worksheet to support the activity. Here are examples of some of the worksheet exercises suggested by GPT-4.o to practice the active and passive voices:

Part 1: Identifying Active and Passive Sentences
Read the following sentences and write whether they are in the active or passive voice.

1. The book was read by the student.
2. They will complete the project by next week.
3. The homework is being done by the children.
4. The chef prepares the meals every day.
5. The song was sung by the choir.

Part 2: Changing Voice
Rewrite the following active sentences in the passive voice.

1. The manager will review the report.
2. The students are writing essays.
3. The company produces innovative products.
4. The artist painted a beautiful mural.
5. The scientist discovered a new element.

Rewrite the following passive sentences in the active voice.

1. The cake was baked by my mother.
2. The letter is being written by John.
3. The car was repaired by the mechanic.
4. The novel was read by millions of people.
5. The presentation will be given by the CEO.

The teacher could work with the tool to refine these before using them with their learners.

The ability of GenAI tools to write code also means language teachers can ask the tools to create interactive games, quizzes, or other language learning materials. These can be embedded in class blogs or HTML readers. Language teachers can input a prompt such as, "Create an interactive quiz for practicing academic words related to scientific report writing" and the GenAI tool will generate code that can be used directly or modified until the desired activity is created (see Figure 6 for an example and Appendix 3 for the HTML code (available online at [short url])). Of course, more specific prompts can be used so the output better reflects the teacher's needs.

Student Using GenAI to Create Materials

Students can work directly with GenAI tools. Language learners can be tasked with creating stories or other texts and inputting the texts into image or video generators and seeing the results. Teachers can give students an AI-generated image or video and ask them to guess the prompt used to create the image or video. Various studies have shown how providing the opportunity for language learners to interact with chatbots can increase their motivation and willingness to communicate (e.g., Chiu et al., 2023; Jeon,

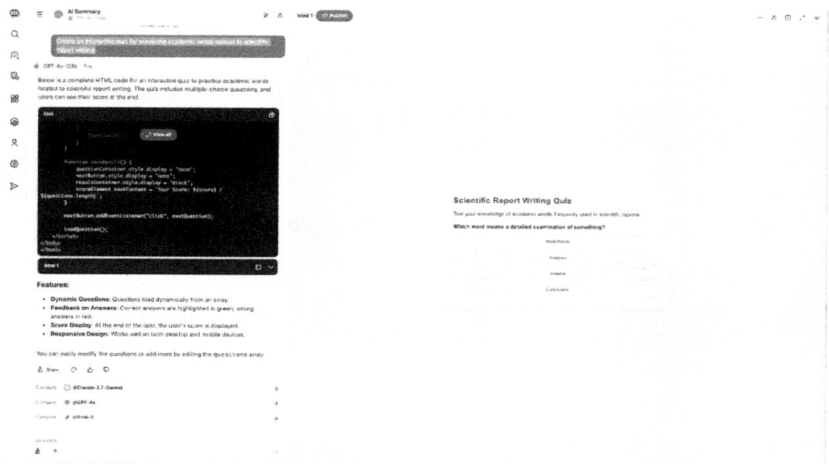

Figure 6 An example of an interactive quiz created on Poe using GPT-4.o

2022). As mentioned in Section 1, rule-based chatbots can only take up pre-programmed roles; however, GenAI-powered chatbots can be prompted to take any role. Language teachers can develop materials (e.g., custom chatbots – see Section 7 for instructions and ideas of how to build custom chatbots) that allow students to interact with conversational AI chatbots in various roles (e.g., famous people (Moorhouse, 2024), tour guides (Javier & Moorhouse, 2023), customer service agents, customers, potential employers), within various scenarios (e.g., job interviews, in a restaurant, getting lost in an unfamiliar city), and communicative purposes (e.g., ordering food, casual conversation, asking for directions). Text-to-voice add-ons or functions can be activated to provide students with oral practice. Moreover, specialist tools such as Call Annie can also be used for conversational practice (Wan & Moorhouse, 2024).

Using GenAI to Create Multilingual Materials

Beyond the previously mentioned possible uses, GenAI tools can support teachers in developing materials that capitalise on students' L1 to support their L2 learning. Although it is well known that strategic use of L1 can assist L2 learning, finding appropriate resources and finding time to create such resources limits their use in the L2 classroom (Kerr, 2014). Moorhouse et al. (2024) found that conversational AI chatbots can be used to develop cross-language comparison activities that could raise learners' awareness of the similarities and differences between their L1 and L2, as well as create multilingual instructions that could help learners and their parents understand task

Generative Artificial Intelligence and Language Teaching

requirements. These tools could be particularly useful for teachers who do not share an L1 with their learners. However, language teachers must declare they have used GenAI tools to assist with the translation of materials.

Conclusion

Lesson planning and preparation can be incredibly time-consuming and challenging for language teachers. Yet, quality planning can lead to more effective language lessons. Similarly, materials tailored to learners' needs will likely be able to assist them in moving their learning forwards. This section has demonstrated ways GenAI tools could assist language teachers in their lesson planning and material preparation. Lesson planning is a great place to start using GenAI as it does not require students to engage with the tools directly, and no sensitive data (e.g., students' work needs to be uploaded to the tools).

Questions for Reflection

1. How might you use GenAI to assist you in creating materials tailored to your learners' needs?
2. How might you utilise the translation capabilities of GenAI tools to create multilingual materials?
3. When might visual, audio, and video generators be useful in your lesson planning and preparation tasks?

4 Using GenAI to Assist with Assessments and Feedback

GenAI-Generated Section Summary

In this section, we asked GPT-4.o to summarise the section as a recipe:

> RECIPE FOR USING GENAI IN ASSESSMENTS, TESTS, AND FEEDBACK
>
> **Ingredients:**
> - 1 clear understanding of assessment types (summative & formative)
> - 3 key assessment characteristics: transparency, validity, reliability
> - A dash of GenAI tools (e.g., ChatGPT, Speechace, Quizbot)
> - 1 teacher's professional judgment
> - A sprinkle of student consent and data protection awareness
> - Optional: Custom AI chatbots

(cont.)

Steps:
1. **Prepare the Purpose**: Define the goal of the assessment (e.g., proficiency, comprehension, feedback).
2. **Design Assessment Tasks**: Use GenAI to generate test items, prompts, or tasks (e.g., multiple-choice, cloze passages). Refine AI outputs for validity and relevance.
3. **Cook with Creativity**: Experiment with prompts to create role-specific scripts, multilingual instructions, or scenario-based assessments.
4. **Grade Smarter**: Upload student work to GenAI tools for grading and feedback. Review AI feedback to ensure tone and accuracy.
5. **Serve Feedback**: Provide actionable, formative feedback using AI-generated suggestions. Customise feedback for individual needs.
6. **Mind the Details**: Respect student copyright, check AI data policies, and keep a "human in the loop" for quality assurance.
7. **Garnish with Transparency**: Communicate openly with students about AI's role in assessments.

Tips:
- Use AI tools to save time but validate results with your expertise.
- Keep assessments meaningful and aligned with learning goals.
- Balance tech efficiency with ethical considerations.

Outcome: A flavorful blend of AI-assisted assessments, tests, and feedback that supports learning while ensuring fairness and reliability.

As you can see, the text is instantly recognisable as a recipe. The conversational AI chatbot identified the key points from the section and included these as ingredients, even including quantities that accurately reflect the section content (e.g., three key assessment characteristics: transparency, validity, reliability). Steps are used to summarise the main points from the section. It could be fun and meaningful to get conversational AI chatbots to change texts from one genre to another and get students to compare the language features and how they relate to their function in a genre.

Introduction

An essential yet challenging task for language teachers is accurately assessing learners' language proficiency and abilities and providing constructive feedback that can help learners move their learning forwards. Although assessments can take many forms, they are often categorised into summative and formative assessments based on the assessment's purpose. Summative assessments are generally used to give an idea of what students can do at a specific time – measuring the product of students' learning (Harmer, 2015). Many standardised language assessments are examples of summative assessments (e.g., IELTS). They provide an example of the learners' attainment against predefined criteria. Formative assessments measure students' learning as part of a process. Instead of measuring what has been achieved, they focus on helping the teacher and learner consider their strengths and areas for improvement (Harmer, 2015). Formative assessment is generally an ongoing process throughout a period of study, while summative assessments usually take place at key milestones (e.g., the end of a teaching unit or course). Assessments can have significant negative and positive impacts on language teaching and learning. Teachers may 'teach to the test' and, therefore, the kind of assessment tasks students are taking can impact directly on instruction. Similarly, students can feel motivated or demotivated depending on their assessment success. This is commonly referred to as the washback effect. Given their impact on language teaching and learning, designing quality assessments is essential.

The quality of an assessment is often judged by three characteristics: transparency, validity, and reliability:

- Transparency: Students and teachers should be made aware of the purpose of the assessment.
- Validity: Assessments should evaluate what they are supposed to assess. For example, a reading assessment should assess students' reading abilities and not other skills, such as spelling.
- Reliability: Assessments should give consistent results. Different assessors should be able to come up with similar scores for the same assessment.

When selecting, designing, marking, and grading assessment tasks with the assistance of GenAI tools, it is important that teachers consider these characteristics. At the same time, there has been extensive discussion about the greater use of technology in assessment practices. Marking and grading assessments can be time-consuming and there can be issues of reliability when many people are involved in the process. Therefore, when ChatGPT was first released, some of the early discussions about GenAI utility in education were about its potential for automatic grading. In an early study involving 12,100 student essays, Mizumoto and Eguchi (2023) found that ChatGPT scored the essays effectively and rapidly in terms of the accuracy of language, potentially saving teachers' time and providing students with quick and informative feedback on their work. Language teachers have also reported using GenAI tools to help them develop assessment tasks for their students (Moorhouse, 2024). There are now a range of specialist online products built on AI technologies that have been designed to assess language proficiencies. For example, Speechace is an online AI speaking assessment tool. Its website suggests it can provide "unbiased, comprehensive, engaging, instant AI spoken English assessment" (Speechace, 2024). It offers reports on pronunciation, fluency, vocabulary, and grammar and aligns the performance with the Common European Framework of Reference for Languages, IELTS, and other international proficiency tests' scoring rubrics. Duolingo and Hallo have similar tests claiming high accuracy rates. Clearly, language assessment and testing are ripe areas for the use of AI tools. Companies see the potential to gain a share of the huge language testing market with valid and reliable automated alternatives to existing proficiency assessments and training programmes.

GenAI-Assisted Assessment Task Design

The analytical and generative capabilities of GenAI tools can assist language teachers with assessment tasks and test item design. Teachers can get suggestions from conversational AI chatbots regarding the kinds of assessments they could use for specific purposes and develop assessment tasks in combination with GenAI tools. Similarly, GenAI tools can be used for automatic item generation (Shin & Lee, 2023). Scholars have already begun to test the potential of various AI tools for creating reading tests. For example, Shin and Lee (2023) conducted a blind test to see if language teachers could identify the difference in the reading passages and testing items extracted from the Korean College Scholastic Ability Test (CSAT) English test, and others generated by ChatGPT. They found no significant difference in how the teachers perceived the naturalness of the flow and expression in the reading passages. However, the participants did find the CSAT test items had more attractive options and were more comprehensive in nature. Kohnke et al. (2023) demonstrated the capabilities of ChatGPT to generate a list of reading comprehension questions for Lewis Carroll's book, *Alice's Adventure in Wonderland*. Similar to the approach used to assist teaching and learning materials development proposed in Section 2, teachers can work with GenAI tools as part of their assessment design and test item development. Teachers first need to consider what the assessment aims to demonstrate (i.e., its purpose), and then work with the GenAI tool to come up with a valid and reliable assessment task. For example, a language teacher may wish to assess students' listening comprehension skills related to a specific social scenario or discourse. The teacher could ask a chatbot to generate a listening script, then modify it to meet their assessment needs. The teacher could then ask the tool to generate multiple-choice comprehension questions that focus on different listening skills (e.g., gist, detail, specific information, etc.). The teacher could record the audio themselves or use a voice simulator to create a listening text. The speech speed could be adjusted to meet the needs of the students. Conversational AI chatbots can also be used to create multilingual instructions for the assessment task or test. It is important that language teachers experiment with different prompts and terms to help them get their desired materials and be specific about the kinds of test items they want to generate (e.g., multiple choice, long answer, short answer, fill-in-the-gap, cloze passage).

To support test item development, there are now a range of specialist tools. Tools such as genQue can generate passages and questions at different proficiency levels related to the CSAT English test. Similarly, Quizbot can be used to generate a variety of question types for PDFs, videos, websites, videos, and audio files, and so on. Conversational AI chatbots can also create similar kinds of test items, although the teacher needs to provide enough contextual information to the tool and carefully check the items generated to ensure they meet the needs of the assessment.

GenAI-Assisted Grading, Analysis, and Feedback

Language teachers often report spending a substantial amount of their time grading, analysing, and giving feedback to their learners' assessment and production tasks. GenAI tools have the potential to support language teachers in their grading, analysis, and feedback work (Godwin-Jones, 2024). Intelligent text editors, such as Grammarly, have been available to help language teachers and learners receive feedback and evaluate language accuracy and appropriateness for some time. These tools were designed for a specific function and could be customised within predefined parameters (Godwin-Jones, 2024). This means users may need to use multiple AI tools to support their language production and evaluation as the features are limited and are "offered in piecemeal fashion, requiring the user to navigate many distinct platforms in order to get assistance" (Tseng & Warschauer, 2023, p. 259). This reduced their utility and, therefore, use in language teaching contexts. However, it does increase the predictability of the tools to complete the predefined task (e.g., providing corrective feedback).

Using conversational AI chatbots provides a greater degree of customisation, but also requires the teacher and learner to have greater knowledge of how to use the tools to get the desired responses. Students' work can be uploaded to the tool and the tool can be prompted to provide a grade and/or feedback on the work based on specific assessment criteria. For example, a university language teacher teaching students how to write a scientific report as part of an English-for-specific-purposes course could input a student's academic writing sample into a conversational AI chatbot to analyse the quality of the work and generate feedback that could assist them in evaluating the work. The teacher could use a prompt such as:

- This is a scientific report submitted by a student for my English-for-specific-purposes course. Please can you analyse the quality of the report and provide feedback on content, language, and structure.

Teachers could also input the assessment rubric into the tool so the tool can provide task-specific evaluation and feedback.

Customised Chatbots and Assessments

GenAI hosting platforms such as Poe allow language teachers to develop custom chatbots and GenAI tools for specific purposes, such as grading using a customised rubric or giving feedback to learners using a specific approach (e.g., feedback sandwich) (Godwin-Jones, 2024; Moorhouse, 2024). Teachers can develop a custom chatbot that provides them with the ability to complete the same task repetitively and more consistently. These platforms also allow the user to refine the prompt and add a specific knowledge base (e.g., task rubric or examples). The customised chatbot can draw upon the knowledge base when providing responses. Teachers need to tweak the prompt or instructions to improve the ability of the chatbot to complete the task.

Formative Feedback

The ability of conversational AI chatbots to take on roles means they can be useful in providing different kinds of formative feedback to learners' production tasks or as part of a task sequence (e.g., process writing). For instance, students might be writing a story; they could be shown how to prompt a GenAI to give feedback in different roles, for example, teacher, reader, or evaluator. In this way, they can find ways to improve the text. Educators have speculated that students may prefer GenAI feedback as they perceive it to be non-judgemental. This could enhance their willingness to engage with the tools as part of their learning processes (see Section 5 for more ideas of how learners can use GenAI in their language learning).

Important Consideration

There are a few things teachers should consider if they plan to use GenAI tools as part of their assessment practices. First, students have copyright over the work they produce. Teachers should get consent from students to input their work into any digital tools. Teachers should check the terms of use of the tools carefully, along with any privacy settings, so they are informed about how any data they input are retained and used. Some tools have addressed this concern. For example, Mizou, a specialist GenAI tool designed for use by teachers, explicitly states that it does not use students' data when training its model. Second, although studies have begun to show how these tools can be accurate in identifying language errors and assessing language (e.g., Mizumoto & Eguchi, 2023), there is still a need for the 'human in the loop' to ensure that the feedback is appropriate to the task, the context, and the learner.

Clearly GenAI feedback offers potential (Barrot, 2023). Studies that compare GenAI and human feedback have shown promising results. Steiss et al. (2024) compared the quality and accuracy of human and ChatGPT feedback. They found humans scored higher in four categories (clarity, accuracy, prioritisation of essential features, and tone); however, ChatGPT feedback was still rated highly in these categories. It excelled in criteria-based feedback. Importantly, there was no difference in the quality of ChatGPT feedback between L2 and L1 writing. It seems that there is indeed potential for using GenAI tools in supporting language teachers' assessment processes; however, due to the sensitive nature of assessment, teachers should consider their professional judgement when using these tools.

Conclusion

Given the significant amount of time teachers dedicate to assessment and feedback, the potential of a tool helping this process is very attractive. However, the use of GenAI within assessment practices is the most controversial use of GenAI in language teaching and learning. It is important that teachers recognise the risks associated with using GenAI in grading and providing feedback, and are transparent with their students on how and why they are using GenAI tools. Accountability and transparency are key to ensuring assessments are seen as valid and reliable. At the same time, reading students' work and providing feedback can help teachers get to know their learners' needs. The next section examines how learners can use GenAI to support their own language learning processes. Guiding learners to use GenAI as part of their feedback-seeking processes can give agency to learners to receive formative feedback on the language learning task at a time conducive to their learning in ways that are most contextualised and helpful.

Questions for Reflection

1. How might GenAI tools help you to design various assessment tasks and test items?
2. What are important factors you need to consider if you wish to use GenAI as part of your marking and feedback practices?
3. How would you feel if you knew your instructors or line managers used GenAI to assess your performance?

5 Students' Use of GenAI in Language Learning

GenAI-Generated Section Summary

For this section, we asked Mapify, a specialised AI tool designed to generate mind maps, to summarise the section as a mind map. It extracted the key information and organised the information into a three-level mind map (see Figure 7).

Presenting content and information in mind maps and infographics can be a way to help language learners visualise language that reflect the kinds of ways they engage with information and knowledge (Kohnke & Jarvis, 2023). Teachers could try using GenAI tools to turn their lesson content into different kinds of infographics and mind maps.

Introduction

This section explores the potential of students using GenAI to support their language learning. It begins by discussing the role of self-directed learning (SDL), a key framework for understanding how students might use GenAI as a technological tool to take control of their learning process. Recognising the affordances of GenAI, students can generate practice exercises, receive instant feedback, or simulate conversations by themselves, tailoring their learning to self-identified needs and desired pace. In this context, fostering *AI literacy* – the ability to discern when and how to use AI effectively – becomes crucial for students. Without this literacy, students may either over-rely on GenAI or fail to leverage its potential in ways that truly benefit their learning. The section includes examples and case studies that explore how we might cultivate AI literacy with students so that they can use GenAI tools to support their own reading, writing, speaking, and listening skills in English. The section helps develop language teachers' competence in preparing students for the GenAI world – a key aspect of

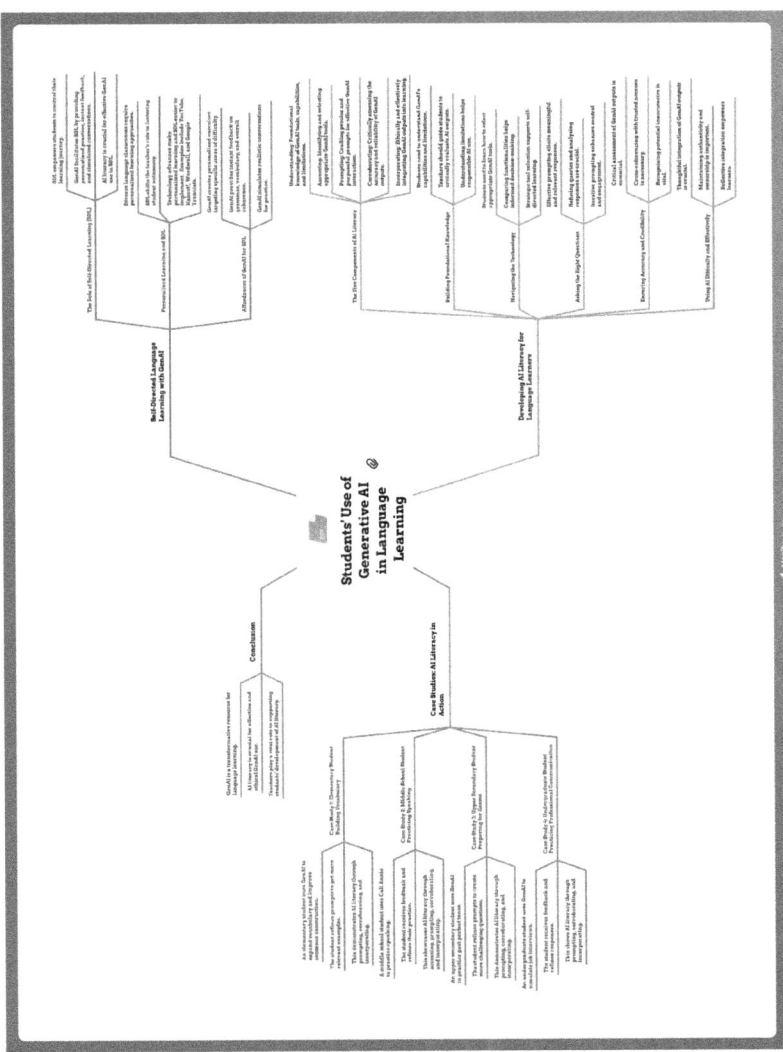

Figure 7 A summary of Section 5 generated by Mapify

P-GenAI-C. In doing so, teachers can support students as they learn to use AI not as a crutch but as a strategic resource in their SDL journeys.

Personalised Learning and SDL

Language classrooms are diverse, with students varying widely in proficiency, interests, and learning profiles. Teachers face the challenge of addressing these differences within the constraints of standardised materials and curricula, which often fail to meet individual needs. This can leave students without sufficient opportunities to practice skills at their appropriate level, leading to frustration and slow progress. To address these challenges, personalised learning and SDL (Zhang & Zou, 2024) have surfaced as promising approaches to meet the unique needs of individual learners. Personalised learning emphasises the teacher's role in designing, differentiating, and adapting learning experiences to meet each student's needs. In contrast, SDL focuses on empowering students to take control over their learning process, shifting the teacher's role to fostering students' ability to learn independently and engage in shaping their own learning path (Palfreyman & Benson, 2019).

Advances in technology have made it easier to implement both personalised learning and SDL. Platforms like YouTube provide authentic input, interactive sites like Kahoot! and Wordwall engage learners with gamified activities (Moorhouse & Kohnke, 2024), and machine translation tools such as Google Translate allow learners to leverage their L1 to support L2 learning (Kerr, 2014). However, many learners are unaware of the many tools available to them or are unsure how to use them effectively. Teachers, therefore, play a critical role in recommending appropriate resources and teaching students how to choose and use different tools to support their learning. This guidance not only personalises the learning experience but also helps students develop the confidence and skills to engage in SDL.

Before the advent of GenAI, tools like rule-based chatbots and writing assistants offered limited support for SDL. Chatbots simulated conversational partners, enabling students to practice speaking, while tools like Grammarly provided personalised feedback to help learners identify areas for improvement (Barrot, 2020; Chiu et al., 2023). These tools allowed students to set goals and adjust strategies based on feedback, aligning with SDL principles. However, their narrow functionality restricted integration into broader teaching practices (Moorhouse, 2024). GenAI tools, with the ability to generate customised practice activities, simulate conversations, and offer instant, detailed feedback, now provide unparalleled support for personalised learning and SDL.

A key element of SDL is self-regulation, which requires students to set clear objectives, track progress, and refine their strategies. Without the ability to self-regulate, learners may struggle to identify their strengths and weaknesses or to maintain long-term motivation. For example, consider a Spanish-speaking high school student with an intermediate level of English who practices conversational English daily to prepare for studying abroad. While motivated, this student struggles to create effective opportunities for practice independently. GenAI tools, which can simulate realistic conversations, generate tailored exercises, and provide immediate feedback, directly address these challenges. By offering accessible, adaptive, and engaging support, these tools empower learners to take greater ownership of their learning journeys. The next section will explore how these affordances make GenAI a powerful resource for SDL learning.

The Affordances of GenAI for SDL

GenAI can support students' self-directed *language* learning by enabling them to create personalised practice exercises, receive instant feedback, and simulate conversations tailored to their individual needs and pace. These affordances can be transformative for learners, especially those who face challenges in accessing traditional language practice opportunities.

First, GenAI allows students to create customised practice exercises that target specific areas of difficulty. For example, if a student struggles with verb tenses and phrasal verbs, they might use GenAI tools to generate targeted grammar drills or vocabulary quizzes designed to address these learning areas. For example, a student could use the following initial prompts with a conversational AI chatbot,

- **Prompt 1**: I am a high school student learning English and I struggle with verb tenses and phrasal verbs. Please create a quiz with 10 sentences where I have to choose the correct verb tense (past, present, or future), and explain why the answer is correct.
- **Prompt 2**: I am a high school student learning English and I struggle with verb tenses and phrasal verbs. Generate five examples of phrasal verbs used in sentences about travel, and give me a definition for each one with Spanish translations.

Second, another critical affordance of GenAI is the ability to provide instant feedback to learners. When a student practices writing, they can input their essays into a GenAI tool that evaluates their grammar, vocabulary usage, and overall coherence according to a rubric. For example, a student might write a short essay about their weekend activities and then prompt the AI to provide feedback. Example prompts include:

- **Prompt 1:** Check this essay for my use of past tense and vocabulary mistakes. Highlight errors, explain why they are wrong, and suggest better alternatives. Then give me a quiz so I can practice the correct past tense form or vocabulary use.

Beyond typed text, some GenAI tools can also analyse handwritten input. Students can take a photograph of their handwritten work and upload it to a chatbot and ask for a digitalised version. Figure 8 shows a handwritten note.

Here is the digitised version of this text generated on GPT-4.o:

Dear Tony,
Thank you for giving me a new soft toy for my birthday. I really like it.
I keep it on my bed. What would you like for your birthday?
Love,
Alice

A student might write an essay or practice grammar exercises by hand, take a photo of their work, and receive instant feedback on errors, legibility, and structure. This immediate feedback loop allows the student to identify patterns in their mistakes (e.g., overusing simple sentence structures) and refine their writing strategies to accelerate their progress. Moreover, this feature bridges traditional learning methods with the benefits of GenAI, ensuring that students can practice language skills in the medium they find most comfortable while still receiving targeted support.

Finally, conversational AI chatbots offer opportunities for simulated conversations, an invaluable resource for language learners who might lack consistent

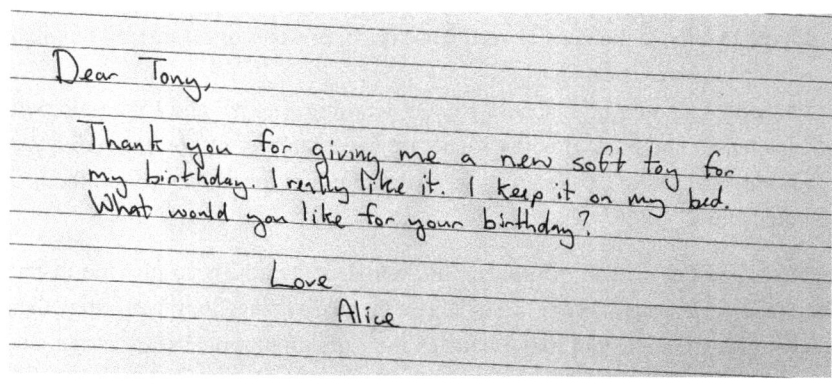

Figure 8 A handwritten note

access to speakers of English. Through AI-driven chat interfaces, language learners can practice speaking in realistic scenarios, such as participating in a class discussion or making travel arrangements. For instance, a student might prompt a conversational AI chatbot to take up a role and engage in role play with the learner. Here are some example prompts:

- **Prompt 1**: Pretend you are a travel agent, and I am booking a flight to New York. Ask me questions about my preferences and respond naturally to my answers.
- **Prompt 2**: Simulate a conversation where I introduce myself to another tourist at an art museum in New York City.

These simulations can be customised to reflect a student's proficiency level and personal interests, making the practice both relevant and engaging. By interacting with GenAI tools, students can build confidence and fluency in a low-pressure environment, bridging the gap between current abilities and personal language learning goals.

Developing AI Literacy for Language Learners

To fully leverage the transformative potential of GenAI in language learning, students must develop AI literacy – a nuanced understanding of how, why, and when to use these tools effectively. AI literacy involves not only technical skills but also the ability to critically engage with the content AI produces, ensuring that it supports meaningful and ethical SDL. Without this critical skill, learners risk misusing AI, such as relying too heavily on it for answers or failing to critically engage with the feedback it provides.

Warschauer and colleagues (2023) offer a helpful five-part pedagogical framework for AI literacy, which includes competencies of understanding, accessing, prompting, corroborating, and incorporating when using AI. This framework provides a structured approach to building AI literacy in learners across age groups and proficiency levels. By fostering these skills, educators empower students with the skills to navigate GenAI tools confidently and responsibly, enhancing their ability to direct their own language learning journeys. The following section first unpacks each of the five competencies and then offers case studies to illustrate how they might apply to language learners.

Understanding: Building Foundational Knowledge

Students must first develop a foundational understanding of the purpose, capabilities, limitations, and ethical considerations of different GenAI tools. Such knowledge is essential for using GenAI as a supportive partner in learning rather than as a substitute for effort or critical engagement. Teachers play a vital role in introducing the strengths and weaknesses of AI tools, encouraging learners to evaluate outputs critically and thoughtfully. For instance, learners might examine how AI performs well with grammatical corrections but may misinterpret context-sensitive language, such as idiomatic expressions or cultural nuances. By understanding these limitations, students build the critical awareness necessary to use AI responsibly and effectively, forming a strong basis for AI literacy.

Accessing: Navigating the Technology

Students must acquire the skills to identify and select GenAI tools that best align with their specific learning objectives. This involves understanding the features of various platforms, comparing functionalities, and making informed decisions based on their goals. For example, a learner seeking to improve oral fluency might evaluate the suitability of Call Annie for conversational practice versus a tool like Speechling for pronunciation refinement. Recognising that certain tools are more appropriate for specific tasks, such as grammar feedback or conversation simulations, helps students approach their learning with a strategic mindset. This process not only enhances their ability to navigate digital resources but also supports their development of SDL skills by encouraging intentional and purposeful engagement with technology.

Prompting: Asking the Right Questions

Interacting effectively with GenAI tools requires learners to craft precise and purposeful prompts that elicit meaningful and relevant outputs. This includes refining queries, analysing responses, and iterating as necessary to ensure the AI-generated content aligns with their learning needs. For example, a language learner may begin by asking for practice sentences using phrasal verbs, then refine the request to include specific purposes or contexts such as travel or business English. This iterative process allows learners to take control of their interactions with GenAI, fostering a deeper engagement with both the language and the technology. Developing the skill to formulate effective prompts is central to building critical thinking and problem-solving abilities, key aspects of both AI literacy and SDL.

Corroborating: Ensuring Accuracy and Credibility

Students must critically assess the accuracy and reliability of GenAI-generated content, particularly for nuanced or complex language tasks. This process involves cross-referencing AI outputs with trusted sources, identifying inconsistencies, and verifying information. For instance, a student analysing a literary text might use GenAI to articulate their own interpretation of the text but compare it against scholarly analyses to ensure the nuances of the original work are preserved. It is also essential to recognise that GenAI tools, while often fluent and confident, can produce incorrect or misleading information, emphasising the importance of independent corroboration. These practices cultivate a habit of critical evaluation, enabling learners to use AI effectively without compromising the integrity of their work or their learning process.

Incorporating: Using AI Ethically and Effectively

Students should thoughtfully and ethically integrate GenAI outputs into their work, ensuring a balance between GenAI assistance and their own contributions. This includes documenting the role of GenAI in their process and ensuring the final product reflects their authentic voice and understanding. For example, when using GenAI-generated suggestions for improving sentence structure, learners should consider rephrasing outputs in their own words, allowing them to internalise and practice the language rather than simply accepting the suggestions verbatim. This approach not only fosters deeper learning but also reinforces ethical practices, promoting transparency and accountability in how GenAI is used to support language learning. Such reflective integration is a crucial component of GenAI literacy and empowers learners to maintain agency and integrity over their educational outcomes.

Applying AI Literacy to SDL Learning

To illustrate how the AI literacy framework can be applied in diverse language learning contexts, this section presents four case studies. These examples demonstrate how learners at different ages develop their understanding, access appropriate tools, craft effective prompts, corroborate AI-generated outputs, and incorporate the results into their language learning processes. By engaging with GenAI tools in purposeful ways, learners build both their language skills and their ability to critically and ethically navigate AI technologies.

> CASE STUDY 1: AN ELEMENTARY STUDENT BUILDING VOCABULARY
> Context: An elementary student in an English immersion program is working to expand her vocabulary. While she learns new words in class, she struggles to use them correctly in sentences and to retain their meanings in different contexts.

CASE STUDY 1: (cont.)

Engagement with AI: After her teacher introduces her to a GenAI tool and explains its limitations, the student begins by prompting: *"What does the word 'excited' mean? Can you give me three sentences using it?"* The AI provides examples like: *"The puppy was excited to see its owner."* While the examples are accurate, the student wants additional context to help solidify her understanding. She refines her prompt: *"Give me three sentences using 'excited' in sentences about this puppy."* This adjustment generates sentences that build on the conversation, align with her interests, and improve her ability to retain and apply the word meaningfully.

AI Literacy in Action: Through these interactions, the student develops her ability to refine prompts (prompting) and critically assess whether the outputs meet her learning needs (corroborating). By reflecting on the examples and using them to create her own sentences, she actively incorporates the AI outputs into her language practice (incorporating). This engagement deepens her understanding of vocabulary use while fostering confidence in navigating AI tools effectively.

CASE STUDY 2: A MIDDLE SCHOOL STUDENT PRACTICING SPEAKING WITH CALL ANNIE
Context: A middle school student learning English as a L2 seeks to improve oral fluency and confidence. However, the student lacks opportunities to practice speaking outside the classroom and often feels self-conscious during group activities.

Engagement with AI: After evaluating several tools, the student selects *Call Annie* for its interactive conversational capabilities. Tools such as Call Annie use avatars to simulate the face of a speaker, increasing the human-like feel of interactions (Wan & Moorhouse, 2024). The student initiates a session by prompting: *"Hi Annie, can we talk about soccer? I want to practice discussing my favorite sport."* Annie engages him in a dialogue, asking questions like: *"What is your favorite soccer team, and why?"* During the conversation, Annie gently corrects his sentences, such as changing: *"I like Messi play"* to *"I like how Messi plays."* At the end of the session, the student prompts: *"Can you summarise the grammar mistakes I made and suggest three sentences I can practice?"* Annie provides a summary and offers tailored practice sentences, such as: *"I enjoy watching Messi play soccer."*

CASE STUDY 2: (cont.)

AI Literacy in Action: By using Call Annie, the student refines his ability to interact effectively with conversational AI (accessing), tailor the interaction to his specific needs (prompting), and assess the relevance and utility of the feedback provided (corroborating). Incorporating these corrections into subsequent practice sessions enhances his oral fluency and confidence, demonstrating how AI can support active, self-directed engagement with language learning.

CASE STUDY 3: AN UPPER SECONDARY SCHOOL STUDENT PREPARING FOR EXAMS
Context: An upper secondary school student in Brazil is preparing for an English proficiency exam. She struggles with complex grammatical structures, particularly the past perfect tense, and wants to focus on improving her accuracy in this area.

Engagement with AI: The student begins by prompting: *"Create five multiple-choice questions about the past perfect tense with detailed explanations for the correct answers."* The AI generates:
Which sentence correctly uses the past perfect tense?

A) *Brazil had gained independence before Dom Pedro I was crowned emperor.*
B) *Brazil gained independence before Dom Pedro I was crowned emperor.*
C) *Brazil has gained independence before Dom Pedro I was crowned emperor.*

The AI explains that the correct answer is A and highlights the importance of sequencing events in the past. Recognising that these questions are useful but not challenging enough, the student refines her prompt: *"Create questions about the past perfect tense using historical events and add detailed explanations for all options."* The revised output provides contextually rich, advanced-level questions tailored to her proficiency.

AI Literacy in Action: This iterative process allows the student to refine her ability to craft purposeful prompts (prompting), critically evaluate the depth and quality of the AI's output (corroborating), and use the generated questions to guide her focused practice (incorporating). These practices not only improve her grammatical accuracy but also equip her with strategies to self-direct her exam preparation.

CASE STUDY 4: AN UNDERGRADUATE STUDENT PRACTICING PROFESSIONAL COMMUNICATION

Context: An engineering undergraduate student preparing for an internship interview seeks to improve her ability to articulate her skills and experiences clearly in English. Although highly proficient, she struggles to structure her responses concisely and confidently in a professional context.

Engagement with AI: The student uses *ChatGPT* to simulate interview scenarios, prompting: *"Pretend you're an interviewer for an engineering internship. Ask me three questions and provide feedback on my answers."* The AI begins with: *"Can you describe a project you've worked on that involved teamwork?"* After responding, the student asks: *"How could I improve my answer?"* The AI suggests adding specific examples of her contributions to the project and using action-oriented language. To further refine her preparation, she prompts: *"Generate three follow-up questions an interviewer might ask based on my response."* This helps her anticipate potential queries and practice responding with confidence.

AI Literacy in Action: Through this engagement, the student learns to tailor AI simulations to her specific needs (prompting), critically evaluate the feedback for relevance and practicality (corroborating), and incorporate the suggestions into her preparation for future interviews (incorporating). This process enhances her professional communication skills while fostering a deeper understanding of how to leverage AI tools for targeted SDL.

Conclusion

This section demonstrates how GenAI can be a transformative resource for language learners, enabling them to personalise their learning journeys while developing essential skills. GenAI tools' abilities to create customised exercises, provide instant feedback, and simulate conversations allow learners to address their unique language needs and goals. By engaging critically with GenAI tools, learners not only enhance their language proficiency but also cultivate AI literacy – a crucial skill for navigating technology in meaningful and ethical ways. Language teachers have an essential role in supporting the development of these skills through modelling effective and EU of GenAI in language learning, while raising learners' awareness of the limitations and critical issues associated with GenAI tools.

When integrated thoughtfully, GenAI empowers learners to take control of their education, fostering SDL and building confidence in their abilities. By using

GenAI tools strategically – as *partners* rather than substitutes – students can bridge gaps in their skills, refine their strategies, and unlock their potential across all language domains. With its flexibility and adaptability, GenAI supports learners in shaping their own educational paths, preparing them for success in an increasingly AI-driven world. In the next section, important ethical concerns are introduced that have implications for how language teachers may use GenAI tools with their learners.

Questions for Reflection

1. How might you model the effective use of GenAI in language learning with the aim of developing students' AI literacy?
2. What capabilities of GenAI might be useful in facilitating your students' language learning?
3. What concerns do you have regarding your students' use of GenAI?

6 Ethical and Social Considerations with GenAI in Language Teaching

GenAI-Generated Summary of the Section

In this section, we asked GPT-4.o to summarise the section as a warning sign to be placed in a teachers' room in a school. The chatbot created a number of warning signs for each aspect of this section. For privity, one example is provided:

⚠WARNING: BIAS IN AI OUTPUTS
- AI tools can reflect *racial, gendered, cultural, or linguistic biases* present in their training data.
- Outputs may marginalise non-dominant varieties of English, reinforce stereotypes, or exclude diverse perspectives.

What to Do:
✔Critically evaluate AI-generated content for fairness and inclusion.
✔Encourage students to analyse and discuss biases in AI outputs.

As you can see from this example, the chatbot extracts the main concerns and advice embedded in the section and re-wrote them as warnings. It added an emoji to emphasise that these are warnings '⚠'. Given that language teaching is a demanding job and we often have limited time to read, asking GenAI tools to create posters and other genres that include key information could be one way to share and reinforce knowledge about AI with colleagues.

Introduction

The advent of GenAI has introduced profound opportunities and challenges in language teaching. However, the desire for efficiency also raises significant ethical and social concerns, prompting educators and researchers to question the broader implications of using GenAI tools for language learning. Issues such as bias, copyright, accuracy, language standardisation, learner motivation, and reduced creativity demand careful examination to ensure that GenAI integration enhances rather than undermines language teaching and learning (Kasneci et al., 2023; Stahl & Eke, 2024).

This section explores the multifaceted and evolving ethical and social considerations associated with GenAI in language teaching. It examines how GenAI impacts language and language learning, highlights key ethical dilemmas such as bias and copyright, and discusses broader social implications like access and environmental sustainability. By addressing these challenges, this section aims to equip educators with important considerations when integrating AI responsibly into their teaching, balancing technological innovation with ethical integrity. In the P-GenAI-C framework described at the beginning of this Element, this section addresses the fundamental aspect of risk, well-being, and EU.

Impact on Language and Language Learning

The widespread use of GenAI in language education has significant implications for how learners engage with and perceive language. While these tools can enhance access to standardised English and support personalised learning, they also risk oversimplifying language use, stifling creativity, and diminishing learners' motivation to engage deeply and productively with the language. This section explores the dual-edged nature of GenAI's impact on language learning, focusing on standardisation, creativity, and motivation.

Standardisation of Language

GenAI tools are primarily trained on large natural language datasets that favor standardised varieties of English, such as Standard American or British English (Smith et al., 2024). This exposure to standard language forms can be beneficial for non-English speakers, as it can provide consistent and largely accepted linguistic models that facilitate global communication (Smith et al., 2024). For instance, learners who lack exposure to specific English-medium settings (e.g., workplace English) can use a chatbot to practice grammar, vocabulary, and sentence construction in contexts that reflect widely accepted norms. Additionally, the standardisation offered by chatbots can help learners prepare for standardised tests like IELTS, where adherence to dominant English conventions is often critical for success. However, while these benefits are important, they may inadvertently undermine the importance of developing communication skills that reflect the diverse, non-dominant contexts where English is also used.

In other words, the dominance of standardised English in GenAI training datasets poses risks of marginalising regional dialects, cultural expressions, and non-standard varieties of English. This standardisation can reinforce linguistic hierarchies, privileging 'correct' or 'proper' forms of English while devaluing others, such as African American vernacular English or regional dialects of Indian English (Milroy, 2001). In language classrooms, tools may overuse certain formal expressions, such as 'delve' or 'commendable', which could homogenise learners' language production and erode opportunities to cultivate individual voice and style (Strokel-Walker, 2024). Moreover, this narrowing effect might discourage learners from embracing linguistic creativity, recognising linguistic diversity, or valuing the richness of their own linguistic and cultural backgrounds, leading to an overly prescriptive understanding of what constitutes 'proper' English (Wan & Moorhouse, 2024).

To address these concerns, educators can take proactive steps to balance the benefits of many conversational AI chatbots' standardised outputs with the promotion of linguistic diversity. Teachers might guide students in critically analysing AI-generated texts, comparing them with regional or cultural variations, and discussing the social implications of language hierarchies. For example, students could examine how a phrase generated by AI might differ from its expression in their local dialect or everyday speech, fostering greater linguistic awareness. This approach encourages learners to appreciate the diversity within English while equipping them with the ability to adapt their language use depending on the audience or context, a crucial skill in global communication. By positioning GenAI as a tool for *exploration* rather than prescription, educators can support students in developing a broader, more inclusive understanding of English as a dynamic and global language. Teachers can also be mindful when selecting voices from voice simulators of ensuring students are exposed to a variety of Englishes.

Creativity and Originality in Language Use

GenAI tools, while helpful in producing polished and fluent text, risk reinforcing formulaic and conventional uses of language (Bai et al., 2023). These tools often rely on patterns derived from LLM training datasets, which can lead to outputs that are predictable and lack the depth of creative nuance offered from people's lived experiences and perspectives. For language learners, this can be particularly limiting, as it may reduce opportunities to experiment with innovative expressions, unique metaphors, or alternative sentence structures. For instance, a learner might rely on a GenAI tool to rewrite a paragraph but receive a result that, while grammatically error-free, lacks the imaginative phrasing that could make their writing distinctive or that fully expresses themselves. Consequently, such reliance can discourage students from exploring their own linguistic creativity, which is essential for developing a personal and authentic writing style, as well as a deep understanding of and appreciation for the language arts discipline.

To mitigate these risks, educators may consider actively encouraging learners to engage in metacognitive reflection about their use of GenAI tools. For example, students could be asked to analyse AI-generated text for stylistic uniformity and then modify it to incorporate more creative, personal, or unconventional elements. This practice not only fosters originality but also cultivates critical thinking about how and when AI should be used as a writing aid. By treating AI as a collaborative *partner* rather than an authoritative source, students can learn to balance the utility of GenAI with the need to develop their unique linguistic voice, ultimately fostering a richer and more individualised, personal, and agentive approach to language use.

Language Learning Motivation

Learner motivation is a critical component of language learning, which has been challenged and requires reconsidering with the integration of GenAI into the language classroom. One concern is that the ease of accessing real-time translation and AI-generated responses could reduce learners' intrinsic motivation to develop their language skills (Stockwell & Wang, 2024). As GenAI tools increasingly provide immediate and polished outputs, some learners might question the value of dedicating time to mastering English, particularly when these tools can seemingly 'do the work' for them (Al-khresheh, 2024; Stockwell & Wang, 2024). This potential decline in motivation is particularly concerning in contexts where learners already struggle to see the practical relevance of language learning.

This dynamic ties closely to Warschauer and colleagues' (2023) 'rich get richer' contradiction, which suggests that technological tools often benefit those already positioned to succeed, while potentially leaving others behind. For motivated learners already proficient in the English language, GenAI offers a powerful way to refine their skills, such as generating advanced-level practice materials or receiving nuanced feedback on writing (Dwivedi et al., 2023). However, for learners with lower motivation or English language proficiency, the same tools might foster overreliance, leading to surface-level engagement and challenges in building foundational language skills (Bai et al., 2023). This disparity risks deepening inequalities in outcomes, as less motivated learners may lack the skills necessary to fully leverage GenAI's potential.

To counter these risks, educators may consider implementing strategies that emphasise the *complementary* role of GenAI in language learning, rather than its replacement of foundational skills. For example, classroom activities can encourage learners to use GenAI tools in specific ways that supports brainstorming ideas or generating focused feedback, but with clear expectations that the final work reflects their own effort, understanding, and words (Moorhouse, 2024). By promoting critical engagement with AI outputs, educators can help learners see GenAI as a tool for enhancing their skills, not replacing them, thereby sustaining their motivation to achieve genuine language proficiency. Furthermore, by integrating reflective exercises that require learners to cognitively engage with GenAI-generated content by evaluating and revising the output, teachers can help reinforce the value of active learning in a world increasingly shaped by AI (Al-khresheh, 2024; Dwivedi et al., 2023).

Ethical Considerations

Using GenAI tools in learning contexts introduces complex ethical considerations that educators and institutions must address. Issues related to bias, copyright, and accuracy are particularly pressing in language teaching, where the implications of these challenges can affect not only pedagogy but also broader notions of fairness, inclusion, and intellectual integrity.

Bias in GenAI

The biases inherent in GenAI tools stem from the datasets used to train them, which often reflect systemic historical inequities and problematic cultural stereotypes. These biases can manifest in language outputs that perpetuate racial, gendered, or cultural prejudices, posing significant challenges to creating inclusive learning environments (Kasneci et al., 2023). For example, a study by Al-khresheh (2024) found that AI-generated outputs disproportionately associated leadership roles with men and caregiving roles with women, perpetuating stereotypes that do not apply to all contexts. Such biases not only affect the quality of the content learners encounter but can also shape their perceptions of societal roles in ways that hinder progress towards equity.

In the language classroom, these biases can influence learners' perceptions of themselves and others, particularly when outputs fail to reflect the diversity inherent in global Englishes. For instance, learners might encounter GenAI-generated dialogues that prioritise Western norms or exclude regional varieties, limiting their exposure to the full spectrum of English use (Milroy, 2001). This exclusion may lead learners to undervalue their linguistic and cultural identities, fostering a perception that their dialects or accents are inferior to standardised forms. Likewise, biases in GenAI may cause learners to perceive their peers from ethnolinguistic minoritised communities as lesser than, warranting a proactive approach to critiquing and engaging with GenAI-generated content in classrooms.

Copyright and Intellectual Property

The question of who owns AI-generated content – whether it is the user, the developer, or the AI tool itself – is a contentious issue. GenAI models are trained on vast amounts of data, much of which may include copyrighted materials used without explicit permission (Lucchi, 2023). This raises ethical concerns about the legality and fairness of using such content, particularly in educational contexts where respect for intellectual property is a core value. Teachers and learners alike may unknowingly breach copyright laws by incorporating AI-generated outputs into their work without understanding their legal status.

This issue extends beyond legality to the principles of academic integrity and attribution. For instance, educators might unknowingly use AI-generated lesson plans or classroom materials derived from copyrighted content without proper acknowledgement. While ChatGPT is able to generate text sets tailored to the linguistic needs of specific learners, the content may be derived from a *New York Times* article, a published poet, or a National Geographic website without permission or consent to use the proprietary work. Similarly, students may incorporate AI-generated essays or translations into their assignments without considering whether the source material was ethically obtained. These practices not only undermine the principles of fair use but also risk setting a precedent where learners view AI-generated content as freely available, diminishing their appreciation for original creation and EU (Lund et al., 2023).

To navigate these challenges, educators must prioritise transparency and ethical practices in their use of AI tools. This includes explicitly teaching students about the importance of copyright laws and the limitations of AI-generated content. For example, educators can have discussions on intellectual property or incorporate lessons on proper citation practices into the curriculum using AI-generated outputs as a starting point for discussions about EU (Draxler et al., 2024). Institutions can further support these efforts by developing clear guidelines that outline the permissible use of AI tools, ensuring that both teachers and learners are aware of their responsibilities when engaging with these technologies. Such measures not only safeguard against legal and ethical missteps but also instil a sense of accountability and respect for intellectual property in the classroom.

Accuracy and Hallucinations

GenAI's capacity to produce fluent and convincing outputs often belies the inaccuracies or what some have called 'hallucinations' embedded within its responses. Hallucinations occur when AI generates incorrect, fabricated, or contradictory information, leading users to mistakenly trust flawed outputs (Walters & Wilder, 2023). These errors can manifest in various ways, from subtle misinterpretations of grammar rules to outright fabrication of facts or citations. For example, a study by Walters and Wilder (2023) revealed that over half of the citations generated by ChatGPT-3.5 in a research paper were either entirely fabricated or contained significant errors, highlighting the potential for misinformation in academic contexts. Large language models rely on statistical probability to generate content, meaning they do not understand the data in their database, nor, do they understand what they generate.

In language learning tasks, inaccuracies in AI-generated outputs can mislead students in understanding the nuances of English usage. For instance, while an AI might produce grammatically correct sentences, it might fail to account for contextual appropriateness or cultural nuances, leaving learners with an incomplete understanding of how language functions in real-world settings. This issue is compounded by the perceived authority of AI tools, where learners may accept the veracity of their outputs without sufficient scrutiny (Kasneci et al., 2023). Such reliance can hinder the development of critical thinking and language skills, which are essential for effective communication.

Educators can play a vital role in mitigating these risks by fostering critical evaluation skills among learners. For example, teachers might design activities where students compare AI-generated content with trusted sources, such as academic texts or grammar guides, to identify discrepancies and discuss their implications. This approach not only helps learners develop a more discerning eye for evaluating content but also equips students with the skills needed to verify information and use AI tools responsibly, ensuring that they are prepared to navigate the complexities of technology-enhanced environments in society.

Social Considerations

The integration of GenAI in education, including language teaching, extends beyond classrooms to broader social implications. These encompass issues such as inequitable access to technology, the shifting roles of teachers in an AI-mediated environment, and the environmental footprint of AI systems. Each of these dimensions highlights the interconnected nature of education and society, illuminating the need for deliberate and ethical approaches to integrating GenAI into teaching practices.

Access to GenAI and Inequity

Access to GenAI tools is not uniform, creating disparities that disproportionately affect learners and educators in under-resourced settings. Many advanced AI systems require subscriptions, limiting their accessibility to individuals and institutions with sufficient financial resources (Lim et al., 2023). This digital divide exacerbates existing educational inequities, leaving marginalised groups unable to fully benefit from the potential of AI-enhanced learning.

For instance, learners in under-resourced regions may rely on outdated or free versions of AI tools that lack the capabilities of their premium counterparts. They might also require fast and reliable internet connections to meaningfully engage with AI platforms. These limitations hinder their ability to access advanced features such as nuanced feedback or real-time conversation simulations, which are critical for language development (Wan & Moorhouse, 2024). Similarly, teachers in resource-constrained settings may lack the training or institutional support to effectively integrate GenAI into their pedagogy, further widening the gap between well-resourced and under-resourced classrooms.

Addressing this inequity requires systemic interventions at multiple levels. Policymakers can advocate for subsidised access to GenAI tools in underserved communities, while institutions can prioritise professional development programs that equip teachers with the skills to use available technologies effectively (Kostka & Toncelli, 2023). Additionally, collaborations between AI developers and educational organisations can lead to the creation of tailored, low-cost solutions that cater to diverse contexts. By taking these steps, educators, administrators, policymakers, and institutions can work towards a more equitable landscape where all learners have the opportunity to engage meaningfully with AI-enhanced language education.

Impact on Employment and Teacher Roles

The rise of GenAI in education has sparked debates about its potential to disrupt traditional teacher roles and reshape the dynamics of the classroom. On the one hand, AI tools can enhance teaching by automating routine tasks such as grading or generating lesson plans, allowing teachers to focus more on individualised instruction and critical thinking activities (Moorhouse, 2024). On the other hand, there is growing concern that over-reliance on AI could diminish the creative and relational aspects of teaching, reducing educators to facilitators of technology rather than active contributors to the learning process.

This tension is particularly evident in the shifting expectations placed on teachers. As GenAI tools potentially take on tasks traditionally associated with content delivery, teachers will be increasingly required to adopt new roles as mediators of technology and guides in critical digital engagement. While these changes present opportunities for dynamic language teaching practices, they also place additional pressure on teachers to adapt quickly to evolving technological landscapes. Still, some studies note that teachers express concerns about job insecurity and a loss of professional autonomy as AI tools become more prevalent (Farrokhnia et al., 2023). To mitigate these risks, it is essential to emphasise the complementary nature of AI in education.

Environmental Impact of GenAI

The environmental implications of GenAI are an often-overlooked aspect of its integration into education and society. Training and deploying LLMs require substantial computational resources, which in turn consume significant amounts of energy. This significantly contributes to the carbon footprint of GenAI technologies, raising questions about their sustainability and long-term viability (Stahl & Eke, 2024). As institutions increasingly adopt GenAI tools for teaching and learning, it becomes crucial to weigh the educational benefits against their environmental costs.

The energy demands of AI systems are particularly concerning given the growing scale and sophistication of generative models. For example, studies indicate that training a single LLM can generate as much carbon dioxide as several cars produce over their entire lifespans (Dwivedi et al., 2023). In educational contexts, the widespread use of these tools – particularly if implemented at scale – could amplify these environmental impacts. Thus, with the proliferation of AI technology in educational contexts, educators and institutions can adopt practices that prioritise specific AI tools that might require less computational power, optimise classroom workflows to reduce unnecessary AI usage, and advocate for greener infrastructure from AI developers. Additionally, incorporating discussions about the environmental impact of technology into the curriculum can raise awareness among students, fostering a culture of responsible and sustainable AI use. By taking these steps, the education sector can contribute to a more balanced approach to technology adoption that aligns with global sustainability goals.

Conclusion

This section has demonstrated that the ethical and social implications of GenAI require careful consideration by language teachers. Issues such as bias, copyright, access inequities, and environmental impact must be addressed to ensure that its integration into education is responsible and equitable.

Teachers play a pivotal role in navigating these challenges. By developing transparent policies, fostering critical engagement, and balancing AI use with human creativity, they can guide learners towards ethical and effective use of GenAI. Moreover, institutional support, professional development, and sustained dialogue among stakeholders are essential to creating an educational environment that embraces the benefits of AI while mitigating its risks. In doing so, educators can empower students not only to achieve language proficiency but also to become thoughtful, informed participants in an increasingly AI-driven world.

Questions for Reflection

1. What risks and ethical issues might be particularly salient in your language teaching context?
2. How might you mitigate these risks and ethical issues when using GenAI tools as part of your professional practices?
3. What guidelines or policies might you implement regarding the use of GenAI in your language teaching context?

7 Essential GenAI Skills and Knowledge

GenAI-Generated Section Summary

In this section, we used GPT-4.o to summarise the section as a 'tweet' for a social media site:

> 🚀 Teachers, unlock the power of GenAI! Learn how to craft effective prompts, validate responses, and tailor tools for your classroom needs. Empower your teaching with essential GenAI skills and knowledge. #EdTech #GenAI #PromptEngineering

We can see how the tool created a text that includes common features of a tweet, like the use of the second person – teachers – to address and capture the attention of the target audience, short catchy sentences to engage the audience, and 'hashtags' to make intertextual references. Creating super-short summaries can help students get the main point of a text, and the use of 'tweets' or other new literacy genres can help learners relate to the writing style and organisation.

Introduction

In this section, essential GenAI skills and knowledge that teachers need to effectively select and interact with GenAI tools are introduced to enhance teachers' P-GenAI-C. Since the release of ChatGPT, there has been a sharp focus on the skills and knowledge needed to work with GenAI tools to generate the desired responses and content. Many of the tools are general models built for generalised uses and not specifically for language teaching and learning purposes. Having this understanding is important, as it helps us recognise why we might not always get the responses we expect – the GenAI does not know our context, role, or task requirements. Therefore, it may be drawing on information irrelevant to our field or task. This means that if we want to be able to utilise GenAI tools in our professional practices, we need to learn how to interact with them. We need the skills and competencies to provide GenAI tools with the information needed to do the task, and, depending on the kind of task we are engaged in, understand that interacting with GenAI tools is an iterative process where we have 'back and forth' conversations until we achieve our desired content or outcomes (Cain, 2023). Importantly, LLMs do not understand language or context, but make statistically informed predictions about the best text to place next in sequence based on the prompt and its training (Cain, 2023).

At the same time, language teachers need some technological knowledge of how GenAI tools work so they can select appropriate tools for their tasks and optimise the settings to meet their needs. Different tools have different sources and training data, along with different processing potential. Teachers can often feel underwhelmed by their interactions with conversational AIs because the models they use might be older or may not be tailored to the settings for their task. Knowledge of how conversational AI tools work can address this issue. There can also be different safeguards, privacy policies, and treatment of copyrighted materials between models that impact teachers' choices of tools. In addition, language teachers need to develop checking and validation processes to verify the information they receive from GenAI tools is trustworthy and legitimate.

Finally, many GenAI tools allow for user tailoring. Language teachers can develop specific chatbots for specific tasks. Tailoring allows for more accurate task performance and consistency. Here the essential skills and knowledge teachers need to use GenAI effectively are elaborated on.

GenAI Interactional Competence

An essential skill is the ability to interact with GenAI tools. This kind of interaction has been called prompting, or prompt engineering (Cain, 2023), but it can also be understood as GenAI interactional competence or prompt literacy (Maloy & Gattupalli, 2024). GenAI interactional competence can be defined as the ability to craft quality prompts and engage in an iterative dialogic process with a GenAI tool until the most relevant and valuable output is achieved (Cain, 2023). Scholars and educators have suggested that implementing well-designed prompts can significantly affect the output generated by GenAI tools (Knoth et al., 2024), and the ability to engage in back-and-forth interactions means that the user can 'refine' or 'expand' on the response through a dialogic iterative process (Cao & Dede, 2023). Maloy and Gattupalli (2024) argue that "prompts are not just the commands we give, but understanding the language that breathes life into ideas, making technology an extension of human intent" (p. 1). Users can tailor the tone or style of the output or request alternative ideas or information (Cain, 2023; Lo, 2023). However, poorly designed prompts can lead to insufficient precision or undesired responses (Knoth et al., 2024).

Cain (2023) argues that teachers need three essential aspects to effectively prompt; 1. content knowledge; 2. critical thinking, and 3. iterative design. Moorhouse et al. (2025) found similar aspects in the prompts used by pre-service language teachers when they engaged GenAI tools as part of their lesson-planning process. Content or pedagogical knowledge allows the user to craft a prompt that includes essential information needed for the GenAI tool to interpret the task. In language teaching, this could include providing information about the learners (e.g., age, proficiency, L1s, interests, needs), teaching objectives (e.g., language points, language skills), teaching methodologies (e.g., task-based language teaching, The Silent Way), and contextual considerations (e.g., lesson length, class size, facilities) that allows the GenAI tool to provide more focused responses, but also allows the teacher to evaluate the content generated by the tool (Moorhouse, 2024).

Next, language teachers need critical thinking. Cain (2023) interprets critical thinking in the context of prompting as the ability to evaluate, verify, and question the generated outputs, as well as being able to detect hallucinations (inaccurate information), biases, or unsuitable responses, and adjust prompts accordingly. In language teaching, this could mean evaluating whether cultures and languages are adequately represented in responses, and whether the suggestions provided are suitable to the learners and teaching context (Moorhouse et al., 2025).

Finally, language teachers need to be able to engage in an iterative design process with the conversational AI chatbot or other GenAI tools to move towards the desired output. Cain (2023) likens this to design thinking, where the teacher starts with a vision and then goes through a process of planning, design, testing, and refinement. Moorhouse et al. (2025) observed this process as pre-service language teachers engaged in lesson planning. Throughout the process, the teachers are actively engaged in decision-making, deciding whether to make further requests, give feedback to the LLM, seek opinions, or ask for refinement depending on their satisfaction with the generated content or response of the LLM.

To craft the initial prompt, various frameworks have been proposed. These include PROPER (Gruber, 2023), CREATE (Birss, 2023), CAST (Jacobs & Fisher, 2023), CLEAR (Lo, 2023), and TRUST (Trust, 2023) frameworks. Although each framework has slightly different suggestions on the components that constitute a good prompt, several key elements are common. These are summarised by Moorhouse (2024) as:

1. Be specific: be as detailed as possible.
2. Include context information: provide background information and include as much data as possible.
3. Use simple language: write in clear and direct language.
4. Give steps: break down complex tasks into steps.
5. Involve iterative and refinement processes: review responses frominitial prompts and engage in back-and-forth conversation until you get the desired content.

Figures 9 and 10 show the difference in responses between a 'poor' prompt and a 'good' prompt. In Figure 9 the prompt used only mentions the genre (short story) and topic (boy in Hong Kong). This means the text is generic and may not meet the language teachers' needs. In Figure 10, the teacher is specific (stating genre, topic) and provides important context information (e.g., reading level). Throughout, simple language is used. The story could be further tailored through a refinement process (e.g., text simplification), change in content, use of specific words of grammar structures, or other changes to meet the teachers' needs. Teachers can also check the content for any biases or stereotyping, making sure the text is appropriate for their learners.

Finding Suitable GenAI Tools for Your Professional Task

Although ChatGPT has received the majority of the attention around GenAI and has even led to terms like 'ChatGPTing', there are several other technology companies who have released GenAI tools (e.g., Anthropic, Meta, and Google). Most of these companies have different models that have different data sources, training data, algorithms, context windows, and parameters. Each of these differences impacts the capabilities, attention, predictability, speed, accuracy,

> **Prompt:** Write a short story about a boy in Hong Kong.
>
> In the bustling streets of Hong Kong, a boy named Kai navigated the vibrant cityscape. Every day after school, he would wander through the narrow alleys of Mong Kok, captivated by the sights and sounds that filled the air. The aroma of street food mingled with the chatter of vendors, creating an enchanting symphony of life.
>
> Kai's favorite spot was a small bookstore tucked away on a quiet corner. The owner, an elderly man named Mr. Chen, always welcomed him with a warm smile. Kai loved to lose himself in the pages of adventure tales, dreaming of far-off places and extraordinary journeys.
>
> One rainy afternoon, as the city shimmered with reflections, Kai discovered an old book with a faded cover. Intrigued, he carefully opened it and found a map tucked inside. It was marked with mysterious symbols and a note that read: "The heart of the dragon lies within."
>
> Excited by the possibility of an adventure, Kai showed the map to Mr. Chen. With a twinkle in his eye, Mr. Chen explained that the map was said to lead to a hidden treasure, a legacy from ancient times.
>
> Fueled by curiosity, Kai decided to follow the map. It led him through the maze-like streets, past bustling markets, and up the steep slopes of Victoria Peak. With each step, he felt a connection to the city he had never experienced before.
>
> Finally, at the top, Kai found a small, overgrown garden. In the centre stood a statue of a dragon, its eyes glinting mysteriously. He knew he had found the heart of the dragon. Though there was no material treasure, he realised the true wealth was the adventure itself and the stories he would share.
>
> As Kai gazed out over the skyline, the city lights twinkling like stars, he felt a profound sense of belonging. Hong Kong was not just a city; it was a living, breathing tapestry of tales waiting to be uncovered. And Kai, with his boundless curiosity, was ready to discover them all.

Figure 9 Example of a poor-quality prompt and response

quality, and relevance of the content generated via the tools. Generally, the more powerful models are only available through subscription, with less powerful models offered for free or as 'freemium' subscriptions. Language teachers need to know some of the technical aspects of GenAI tools so they can make informed decisions about the tools and understand why they perform the way they do. As many specialist AI tools are also built on different GenAI models, it

Generative Artificial Intelligence and Language Teaching

> **Prompt**: Write a short story about an unbelievable day a ten-year-old boy had in Hong Kong. It should include an unexpected twist and a funny resolution. The text should have a Flesch reading score of 70.0-80.0 for a US 7th grade student. The story should be 200 words long.
>
> **An Unbelievable Day in Hong Kong**
>
> Tommy, a curious ten-year-old, woke up excited in Hong Kong. Today was the big dragon boat festival! He raced downstairs, gulped his breakfast, and dashed to the harbor.
>
> As he watched the colorful boats, a shiny object bobbed in the water. Curious, Tommy leaned closer, slipped, and splashed right in! Gasping, he grabbed the object—a golden compass.
>
> Suddenly, everything around him changed. The bustling harbor turned into an ancient village, and the boats were now giant, talking fish! One fish, named Finley, said, "Welcome, traveler! You must find the Golden Pearl to return home."
>
> Tommy, both scared and thrilled, agreed. With Finley's help, he navigated through markets, dodged mischievous monkeys, and finally reached a hidden cave. Inside, they found the Golden Pearl guarded by a sleepy dragon.
>
> Tommy remembered the dragon loved music. He played a tune on his phone, and the dragon swayed, then snoozed. Quickly, Tommy grabbed the pearl and the compass glowed.
>
> In a flash, Tommy was back at the harbor, soaked but smiling. He laughed, realising he'd been dreaming. But when he reached into his pocket, the pearl was still there—a funny reminder of his unbelievable day!

Figure 10 Example of a good-quality prompt and response

can also be helpful for teachers to understand the strengths and limitations of these tools, too. Here the terms are briefly introduced:

1. Data source: data source refers to the origin or collection of information from which training data are derived. It is the raw, unprocessed information that may be used to create training data. Data sources can include: books, articles, academic papers, web pages, social media posts, government documents, transcripts of spoken language, code repositories, and databases. Data sources are typically vast and may contain information in various formats, not all of which will necessarily be used in training. Some companies have signed agreements with newspapers and publishers to gain access to their archives as source data and training data for their GenAI models.

2. Training data: training data is the processed, curated, and formatted dataset actually used to train the LLM. It is derived from data sources but has undergone several steps of preparation:

- Cleaning: removing irrelevant information, correcting errors, and standardising format
- Tokenisation: breaking text into smaller units (tokens) that the model can process
- Formatting: structuring the data in a way the model can understand and learn from
- Balancing: ensuring a good representation of various topics, writing styles, and so on
- Filtering: removing inappropriate or low-quality content.

GenAI companies do not release much information on the training data but it is likely that each model will have different data within its dataset. By asking different conversational AI chatbots for the same information, you can see variations in their data sources. For example, we asked several chatbots to write a short biographical statement about Benjamin Luke Moorhouse using the prompt: "Write a short biographical statement about Dr Benjamin Luke Moorhouse." The responses are presented here:

- GPT-4.o: Dr. Benjamin Luke Moorhouse is a distinguished academic and researcher specialising in [insert area of expertise, e.g., education, linguistics, science, etc.]. With a passion for advancing knowledge and fostering innovation, Dr. Moorhouse has contributed significantly to his field through his research, publications, and teaching. He is known for his commitment to mentoring students and his dedication to bridging the gap between theory and practical application. Dr. Moorhouse continues to make impactful contributions to [specific field or discipline], inspiring both colleagues and learners alike.
- Claude 3.5 Sonnet: Dr Benjamin Luke Moorhouse is an Assistant Professor at The Education University of Hong Kong, specialising in English language teaching and teacher education. His research focuses on technology in language education, pre-service teacher preparation, and mentoring in teaching practicum. He has made significant contributions to understanding how technology can be effectively integrated into language teaching and learning, particularly in the Hong Kong context. Dr Moorhouse has published extensively in academic journals on topics related to English language education and teacher development. He is also known for his work on supporting student teachers during their teaching practice experiences. Would you like

me to elaborate on any particular aspect of Dr Moorhouse's work or background?
- GPT-4o1-mini: As of my knowledge cutoff in October 2023, I do not have specific information about Dr. Benjamin Luke Moorhouse. It's possible that Dr. Moorhouse is a faculty member specialising in a particular academic field at the university. For the most accurate and up-to-date biographical information, I recommend visiting the university official website or contacting the university directly.

Different models gave different responses. GPT-4.o provided a generic template. Claude 3.5 Sonnet gave a more specific statement but with inaccurate information (e.g., a wrong affiliation), while GPT-4o-mini replied that it did not have specific information about Dr Benjamin Luke Moorhouse and the user should visit his university website. This shows how the size and scope of the dataset differs between models. As the datasets are constantly being added to, the information provided can also change over time. It is also important to remember that texts that are copyrighted or behind 'paywalls' may not be included in datasets, which can have an effect on the content produced.

3. Parameters: parameters are the adjustable values within an LLM that the model learns during training. They can be thought of as the 'knowledge' or 'skills' of the model. Parameters determine how the model processes input and generates output. Generally, more parameters allow for more complex relationships and potentially better performance, though this is not always true. Most LLMs can have billions of parameters (e.g., GPT-3 has 175 billion).
4. Context window: the context window is the number of tokens the model can consider at once when generating a response. It determines how much previous text the model can use to understand context and generate relevant responses. So, if your prompt is too long, or you have a long interaction, you might exceed the context window and the GenAI will 'forget' parts of the conversation or prompt. Large language models sometimes indicate the context window by stating the maximum number of tokens (words or word pieces) the model can process in a single operation (e.g., Claude 3.5 Sonnet – 200,000). A larger context window can slow down the speed of the LLM but allow for a longer coherent interaction.
5. Temperature: temperature is a setting used during the text-generation process that affects the randomness of the model's outputs. It is represented by a value (usually between 0 and 1) that controls the randomness of the model's token selection. A lower temperature (e.g., closer to 0) will generate more deterministic, focused, and conservative outputs, while a higher

temperature (e.g., closer to 1) will generate more random, diverse, and creative outputs. It allows more fine-tuning of the model's behaviour for different tasks without the need for retraining.
6. Algorithms: an algorithm is like a set of step-by-step instructions that tells a computer how to do something. Algorithms in GenAI are the detailed instructions and rules that guide computers in learning from existing data and then creating something new. They tell the AI how to:

- Learn from data: analyse and understand patterns, structures, and styles in the information it's given (like thousands of images or sentences).
- Generate new content: use what it has learned to produce original material that resembles the learned data but isn't a copy of it.
- Improve over time: continuously refine its creations by comparing them to desired outcomes and adjusting accordingly.

Different GenAI tools will have different algorithms determining how the tools respond to the user's prompts and interactions. These algorithms are influenced by the AI company's values, beliefs, and unconscious biases.

Before using a GenAI tool, teachers are advised to note the model, features, and settings of the tool to better understand the tool's performance in the GenAI process. If settings are adjustable, teachers can try out different settings and see the impact on the content. They can also try different GenAI models with the same prompts to discern differences in how the tools treat the prompt. Through experimentation, teachers can better understand the models, features, and settings that best help them in their professional practices.

Corroborating and Validation of GenAI Content

As detailed in Section 6, the content and responses generated by GenAI tools are not always accurate, the reliance on statistical probability, even when they have received extensive training, means they can 'misinterpret' the user's prompt and generate inaccurate information, or information that is biased. Teachers should assess the content generated that could teach or reinforce biases or stereotypes. This seems particularly important for language teachers working in multicultural and multilingual environments using GenAI tools that have Western and English biases and less oversight of content generated in languages other than English. To avoid this, teachers can:

1. Use common sense: the first process is to use common sense. The teacher can review the content generated and consider if it makes sense based on their existing knowledge. They can think about whether the content is biased

or contains stereotypes that might be harmful towards students in their class or reinforce existing biases.
2. Try the same prompts in other GenAI tools: as different tools have different datasets and algorithms, they will generally generate different content to the same prompts. Teachers can submit the same prompt to two or more chatbots, and if the responses are similar and consistent across chatbots, it likely means the content is valid. To test this suggestion, teachers could use the prompt: "List the top three tourist attractions in [a city/country]" and input it in different LLMs. We tried this with the city of Hong Kong:

- o1-preview: 1. Victoria Peak; 2. The Star Ferry and Victoria Harbour; 3. Tian Tan Buddha (Big Buddha); and Po Lin Monastery.
- Claude 3.5 Sonnet: 1. Victoria Peak; 2. Tian Tan Buddha (Big Buddha); 3. Victoria Harbour.
- Gemini-1.5-Pro: 1. Victoria Peak (The Peak); 2. Hong Kong Disneyland; 3. Tian Tan Buddha (Big Buddha); and Po Lin Monastery.

This example demonstrates how three different GenAI models are relatively consistent in recommending tourist attractions in Hong Kong. Victoria Peak and Tian Tan Buddha appear in all three responses, with only Gemini-1.5-Pro suggesting Disneyland. Teachers can be confident that Victoria Peak and Tian Tan Buddha are two of the top tourist attractions and could do further research on Victoria Harbour and Hong Kong Disneyland if needed.

3. Check sources cited in a chatbot response: sometimes teachers may be working with a chatbot to write reports or other academic or technical documents. The chatbot may provide citations to reference relevant sources. These can look real but may be fake or inaccurate. Teachers can check the accuracy of the cited source by using Google Scholar, SCOPUS, or other search engines (e.g., Consensus). It is important that even if the source exists, teachers check if the source supports the points provided in the chatbot's response.
4. Use other 'authoritative' sources to verify the content: teachers can check the content by conducting searches on the internet or referring to books. Teachers can use academic journals, newspapers, government websites, or documents, and so on. However, it is important to remember these sources can also contain biased and inaccurate information and may represent a specific world view or a particular author's agenda.

The development of GenAI reminds us of the importance of information literacy and the need to be critical when we engage with any texts, those generated by GenAI, and those generated by humans. Developing checking and validation processes can aid teachers in ensuring they provide accurate information to their learners.

Tailoring Chatbots for Your Tasks

At the beginning of this section, we mentioned that many GenAI tools have been built for general purposes, not specifically for language teaching and learning. Although there are now specialist tools built on LLM infrastructure designed specifically for teaching and learning purposes (e.g., MagicSchool), many LLMs allow customisation by users so they can create tools for specific teaching and learning tasks (e.g., providing formative feedback, providing information about words, acting as a critical friend for advice on teaching ideas and materials) (Moorhouse, 2024). Poe, a platform that includes various GenAI tools, allows users to create their own 'bots' and customise the settings. First, users can select a 'bot type' such as prompt bot, image generator, video generator, role play, and server bot. After selecting an appropriate bot, the bot can be given a name, a base bot (e.g., ChatGPT) can be selected, instructions can be inputted, and a specific knowledge base can be uploaded. Teachers can 'tweak' the instructions and test the responses until the bot can consistently complete the task. Knowledge bases can make the bot provide more specialised responses (e.g., curriculum materials, syllabi, course materials, marking, or feedback rubric).

A teacher may want to provide their learners with a customised bot that can provide detailed information about the words they are learning with explanations in the learners' L1s. Using a general LLM would likely mean the teacher would need to provide students with some prompt training and even then, the content produced may not be consistent. Instead, they can tailor an LLM issuing the 'create bot' function. In this way, the students can interact with the tailored bot for the specific task of looking up new words. Other GenAI tools like Perplexity also allow for customisation.

Conclusion

GenAI tools generally have intuitive interfaces, and it is relatively easy to use them: just input a prompt and get a response. However, to use the tools effectively and responsibly for specific professional tasks requires more advanced knowledge and skills. This section provided an overview of some fundamental skills and knowledge language teachers need to use these tools in all aspects of their professional roles. As technology becomes more complex, users generally become less aware of their inner workings. Many people may be able to change the oil in a petrol car, but probably have no idea how to conduct any maintenance on an electric car. This means that if teachers want to be critical and responsible users, they need some basic knowledge and understanding. This allows them to select appropriate tools, interact with GenAI effectively, check the content the GenAI tools create, and tailor the tools to their needs.

Questions for Reflection

1. Which prompting framework do you find most useful for your interactions with GenAI tools?
2. How have your interactions with GenAI changed after reading this section?
3. What ways do you use to check and verify the content generated by GenAI tools?

8 Enhancing Professional GenAI Competence through Professional Development

GenAI-Generated Section Summary

In this section, we asked GPT-4.o to summarise the section as a restaurant menu. We have just included the main courses here as an example:

Main Courses

Self-Directed Learning Salad 🥗
- A fresh mix of GenAI tools, micro-learning resources, and actionable goals.
- Topped with examples of prompt engineering and step-by-step learning strategies.

Community Collaboration Casserole 🥘
- A hearty dish of teacher communities, both local and online, seasoned with peer support and shared practices.
- Served with a side of student involvement for added flavor.

Reflexive Research Risotto 🍚
- A rich blend of reflective practice and practitioner research.
- Features action research "grains" and a dash of low-stakes experimentation.

We thought a menu might reflect the section theme of professional development and how we can pick and choose what and how we learn given the wide variety and easily accessible development options. We were impressed with the GenAI's ability to come up with catchy names for the dishes on the 'menu'. Lots of wordplay, such as, alliteration.

Introduction

The development of GenAI tools creates a need for language teachers to revisit their professional skills and knowledge. Technological advances continuously change human practices, which in turn change the knowledge we need to successfully engage in these practices. New technologies will at first disrupt our current understanding and often lead to 'pushback' as we need to shift our way of doing and thinking. Early adopters will see the potential of these technologies, but it takes longer for a community as a whole to adapt. Yet, over time, these technologies will become normalised and part of our professional expectations (Bax, 2003). This creates new 'cultures of use' within professional communities – the commonly shared norms and forms of activity adopted by members of a group or community when using technologies (Thorne, 2003). A specific profession may use technology differently than other professions. Previous examples of technologies that have become normalised within language teaching include presentation tools, interactive whiteboards, student response systems, and learning management systems (Moorhouse & Yan, 2023). As stated in the Introduction, this Element was centred on the idea that language teachers need P-GenAI-C to competently and responsibly use GenAI in their professional practices. This Element has detailed the kinds of knowledge and skills language teachers would need to develop P-GenAI-C, however, as GenAI tools are constantly advancing, we want the concluding section to be future-focused, considering how GenAI may shape language teaching in the future. The final section also provides suggestions for ways teachers can continue to enhance their P-GenAI-C through engaging professional development.

Looking Forward

It is becoming increasingly difficult to predict the future. Even since we began writing this Element, new GenAI tools have been released with new capabilities. The impact of these tools on language teaching and learning are only just starting to be realised. Yet, the rapid embedding of AI assistive features in digital tools, including educational technologies (e.g., learning management systems) suggests that AI will be rapidly adopted into language teachers' practices. Futurists are predicting that in the near future, there will be AI teachers operating as autonomous AI agents who can personalise their instruction to the needs of individuals. The first 'teacherless' AI school opened in London, UK, in 2024. GenAI, robots, VR and augmented reality, and avatar technologies can be combined to create 'interactive virtual teachers' where students can engage with them in real time in the Metaverse. Virtual reality already shows promise in language teaching. Dooley et al. (2023) found that young language learners produced more examples of spontaneous language use, increased mediation between learners, and higher levels of production and comprehension than expected. Combined with 'non-judgemental' GenAI avatars, students might feel even more willing to communicate in their target language. These avatars can act as a language coach and conversational partner, and take up any role in role-play activities. Teachers can capitalise on the GenAI VR environment to better personalise the learning experiences for diverse learner groups (Moorhouse et al., 2023).

In the near future, teachers will be able to virtually clone themselves, providing a way for learners to get support 24/7 from a familiar face. Heygen launched the 'virtual twin', which they argue can join meetings on the user's behalf. These developments are causing legitimate concern for many, due to obvious ethical concerns but also due to the worry they will be replaced. However, humans are inherently social beings who like to come together for common goals – for example, learning. It seems then that GenAI will likely augment language teaching, making possible professional practices previously seen as challenging (e.g., personalised learning), but keeping the human language teacher as a central part of a learning environment.

We predict that the general AI models that are now common will be replaced with more personalised models that will understand our needs and be more tailored to our contexts. This will further increase their utility in our work. We also predict that developing P-GenAI-C will be a requirement for language teachers in the near future, and there will be a need to continuously refine competencies as the technologies progress and new methodologies are developed. At the same time, as tools become more specialised, the control the user may have over them could become diminished (Darvin, 2025). Current tools designed specifically for teaching, for example, MagicSchool and Twee, while providing easy to use interfaces that can make it easy for teachers to efficiently find a template and tool to create a desired response, also reduce the control the user has to interact with the content created and refine their ideas through an iterative process (Chen et al., 2024). At this stage, teachers should explore the use of general GenAI tools (e.g., conversational AI chatbots) and develop their GenAI interactional competence so they can maintain more control over the content they create.

More than ever, language teachers will need to be able to monitor their own P-GenAI-C and find ways to develop themselves to stay relevant in the GenAI age. We advocate for self-directed, community-orientated, evidence-informed, reflexive professional development. When teachers see a need to develop, they will be more dedicated to it. When they have a supportive community, they will likely sustain their development. When the development is evidence-informed and reflexive, teachers are likely to see positive outcomes to their development and make adjustments based on the context.

Self-Directed Professional Development

Stockwell and Wang (2023) remind us that, while teachers have a responsibility to facilitate their students' language learning, "teachers are human, and are learners of technology themselves" (p. 479). Technology has enabled teachers to access a large range of professional development opportunities in various modalities. GenAI has increased these opportunities. Section 2 illustrates how GenAI tools can be used to help develop teachers' topic and content knowledge development, gain an understanding of language-teaching methodologies and approaches, and build awareness of languages, cultures, and societies. These can be incredibly useful when combined with the checking and validation processes proposed in Section 7 in helping language teachers develop professionally.

Along with using GenAI tools, language teachers can access various micro-learning resources and activities. Micro-learning activities are designed to break topics into short, concise, and easily consumable segments ('chunks') of learning (Kohnke et al., 2024). Micro-learning activities are usually short and multimodal, incorporating videos, animations, and infographics (Reinhardt & Elwood, 2019). They deliver personalised, timely, and SDL activities (Kohnke, 2023). Kohnke and Moorhouse (2024) found that language teachers often value the opportunity to acquire knowledge and skills through micro-learning activities, which foster experimentation without causing cognitive overload. To engage in micro-learning, language teachers need to first identify an area for improvement (e.g., writing more effective prompts). They would then seek out relevant resources like video-hosting sites (e.g., Youtube), social media sites (e.g., LinkedIn Learning), or relevant apps (e.g., Duolingo), and engage with the content to achieve their learning goal. Developing clear and narrow learning goals means that the materials sourced can be more focused and the learning easier to measure. For example, "Learn how to build a customised GenAI tool for language teaching purposes" is a better goal than "Learn about GenAI tools".

In addition to micro-learning, various platforms offer short courses that provide micro-credentials that teachers can use to receive recognition for their learning. Google and Microsoft both offer learning platforms that can lead to accreditation. Microsoft has the 'AI learning hub' that includes a range of self-access learning units on different aspects of AI knowledge and skills. They also have 'AI for Education' resources and courses that are tailored to teachers. Google offers courses on AI in education, including 'Generative AI for Educators'. LinkedIn Learning offers a range of educational development resources created by different companies and content creators.

As it becomes easier to create content designed to promote teacher development, we need to carefully consider the quality of such courses and resources. Language teachers need to be critical of the professional development they receive and consider its utility in their context. Greater emphasis needs to be placed on developing teachers' ability to engage in practitioner research, so they can implement context-specific technological innovations, monitor their implementation, and evaluate their effectiveness.

Community-Orientated Professional Development

Language teachers around the world are all trying to understand how to best adapt to the development of GenAI tools. By coming together with other educators and education stakeholders, teachers can learn from each other within a community-orientated approach. A community-orientated approach provides teachers with support, guidance, mutual understanding, and critical friends as they try to navigate new realities and develop the competencies needed to support their language learners. It allows teachers to position themselves within a larger system with shared common aims but with different, yet equal, contributions.

Language teachers can create learning communities in their schools, districts, professional organisations, and beyond. These communities do not need to be restricted to language teachers alone, instead, they can involve students, parents, and other key stakeholders, ensuring different voices can be learned from. Organising sharings of practices, raising concerns on the impact of GenAI for discussion, and exploring new features and tools as a group can help teachers to feel more supported and confident to try them out in practice. Social media platforms, such as 'X', 'Bluesky', Facebook, and LinkedIn have a large number of 'virtual communities' where teachers can learn from and engage with colleagues around the world.

At the school level, the community can involve students, especially if any changes to practice affect their learning. Students can be invited to be involved in different levels of decision-making, curriculum design, learning activity preparation, and assessment practices as teachers and schools adapt to GenAI developments. Student–teacher consultation groups can be established, and students can be invited to participate in professional development events.

Evidence-Informed and Reflexive Professional Development

The ability to reflect on our lived experiences allows us to better understand ourselves and our actions, leading to continuous adaptation and learning.

Dewey is widely credited for highlighting the importance of experiential learning and reflective thought as the "sole method of escape from the purely impulsive or purely routine action" (1933, p. 15). Technological developments can be a catalyst for reflection, as they force us to challenge our current way of thinking and doing, and 'complicate' the status quo. As new technologies become embedded in professional practices, we can often lack evidence to their effectiveness on different aspects of learner outcomes. In addition, language teaching is highly context-specific, requiring localised evidence to support the adoption of specific technologies or practices into the classroom (Richards, 2010).

Language teachers are encouraged to engage in practitioner research, through self-study, reflective practice, or action research methodologies to explore the use of GenAI tools in their professional practice. Teachers can start with implementing GenAI tools into low-stake professional tasks, such as lesson preparation and planning. Lesson preparation is conducted out of the classroom and away from students, reducing the pressure on teachers. Language teachers can spend time experimenting and refining their practices and see if GenAI has positive impacts on their preparation processes. Teachers can keep a diary of their experimentations to help them critique and reflect upon their exploration. Teachers should recognise this process of learning can be messy and increase their sense of vulnerability – but this is a perfectly normal part of learning. Teachers could then explore how GenAI could be used to assist specific pedagogical practices (see Sections 3–5 for inspiration). Teachers can collect artefacts, invite colleagues to observe and provide suggestions, and gather feedback from learners and parents to provide a more holistic view of the explorations.

Over time, teachers can build use cases that could be invaluable to the wider language teaching community. Language teaching conferences and organisations (e.g., TESOL International Convention, RELC International Conference, AILA World Congress) can be valuable spaces for the sharing of use cases and empirical research into the use of GenAI in language teaching. By actively engaging in the wider language teaching community, teachers can be exposed to and contribute to shaping the communities' response to GenAI developments.

Conclusion

In this final section, we postulated about the future of GenAI in language teaching. Clearly, this is a revolutionary technology that has been rapidly adopted into various processes. It is important that language teachers and their students maintain agency over whether and how these tools are used (Darvin, 2025). As Godwin-Jones (2022) mentions, technology should be seen as part of a variety of human and non-human resources that teachers can draw upon to help learners achieve their language learning goals. To do this, though, language teachers need to continuously develop their P-GenAI-C, so they have the knowledge needed to critically evaluate and reflect on the use of GenAI in language teaching and learning.

Questions for Reflection

1. If you haven't used GenAI in your language teaching before, how might you start using it? How might you collect evidence on the effectiveness of your GenAI use?
2. What aspect of P-GenAI-C would you like to develop further? How might you use micro-learning to support your development?
3. What are your predictions for the future of GenAI? How will you prepare yourself for the future?

References

Al-khresheh, M. H. (2024). Bridging technology and pedagogy from a global lens: Teachers' perspectives on integrating ChatGPT in English language teaching. *Computers and Education: Artificial Intelligence*, 6, 100218. https://doi.org/10.1016/j.caeai.2024.100218.

Ali, O., P. A. Murray, M. Momin, Y. K. Dwivedi, & T. Malik. (2024). The effects of artificial intelligence applications in educational settings: Challenges and strategies. *Technological Forecasting and Social Change*, 199, 123076.

Bai, L., X. Liu, & J. Su (2023). ChatGPT: The cognitive effects on learning and memory. *Brain-X*, 1(3), e30. https://doi.org/10.1002/brx2.30.

Baker, W. (2012). From cultural awareness to intercultural awareness: Culture in ELT. *ELT Journal*, 66, 62–70. https://doi.org/10.1093/ELT/CCR017.

Barrot, J. S. (2020). Integrating technology into ESL/EFL writing through Grammarly. *RELC Journal*, 53(3), 764–768. https://doi.org/10.1177/0033688220966632.

Barrot, J. S. (2023). Using ChatGPT for second language writing: Pitfalls and potentials. *Assessing Writing*, 57, 100745. https://doi.org/10.1016/j.asw.2023.100745.

Bauml, M. (2014). Collaborative lesson planning as professional development for beginning primary teachers. *The New Educator*, 10(3), 182–200.

Bax, S. (2003). CALL: Past, present, and future. *System*, 31(1), 13–28.

Birss, D. (2023) How to research and write using generative AI tools. *LinkedIn Learning*, formerly Lynda.com. www.linkedin.com/learning/how-to-research-and-write-using-generative-ai-tools.

Bonner E., R. Lege & E. Frazier (2023). Large language model-based artificial intelligence in the language classroom: Practical ideas for teaching. *Teaching English with Technology*, 23(1), 23–41. https://doi.org/10.56297/bkam1691/wieo1749.

Brown, T., B. Mann, N. Ryder, M. Subbiah, J. D. Kaplan, P. Dhariwal, & D. Amodei (2020). Language models are few-shot learners. *Advances in Neural Information Processing Systems*, 33, 1877–1901. https://proceedings.neurips.cc/paper_files/paper/2020.

Cain, W. (2023). Prompting change: Exploring prompt engineering in large language model AI and its potential to transform education. *TechTrends*, 68(1), 47–57. https://doi.org/10.1007/s11528-023-00896-0.

Cao, L. & C. Dede (2023). *Navigating a World of Generative AI: Suggestions for Educators*. The Next Level Lab at Harvard Graduate School of Education.

https://bpb-us-e1.wpmucdn.com/websites.harvard.edu/dist/a/108/files/2023/08/Cao_Dede_final_8.4.23.pdf.

Chan, C. K. Y., & T. Colloton (2024). *Generative AI in Higher Education: The ChatGPT Effect*. Routledge.

Chen, Z., T. Liu, & X. Liu (2024). *Twee*: Artificial intelligence assistant to generate versatile materials for language education. *RELC Journal*. https://doi.org/10.1177/00336882241282471.

Chiu, T. K., B. L. Moorhouse, C. S. Chai, & M. Ismailov (2023). Teacher support and student motivation to learn with artificial intelligence (AI) based chatbot. *Interactive Learning Environments*, 32(7), 3240–3256. https://doi.org/10.1080/10494820.2023.2172044.

Crompton, H., & D. Burke (2024). The educational affordances and challenges of ChatGPT: State of the field. *TechTrends*, 68, 380–392. https://doi.org/10.1007/s11528-024-00939-0.

Darvin, R. (2025). The need for critical digital literacies in generative AI-mediated L2 writing. *Journal of Second Language Writing*, 67, 101186. https://doi.org/10.1016/j.jslw.2025.101186.

Dewey, J. (1933). *How We Think: A Restatement of the Relation of Reflective Thinking to the Educative Process*. D. C. Health and Company.

Dooley, M., T. Thrasher, & R. Sadler (2023). 'Whoa! incredible!': Language learning experiences in virtual reality. *RELC Journal*, 54(2), 321–339. https://doi.org/10.1177/00336882231167610.

Draxler, F., A. Werner, F. Lehmann, M. Hoppe, A. Schmidt, D. Buschek, & R. Welsch (2024). The AI ghostwriter effect: When users do not perceive ownership of AI-generated text but self-declare as authors. *ACM Transactions on Computer-Human Interaction*, 31(2), 1–40. https://doi.org/10.1145/3637875.

Dwivedi, Y. K., N. Kshetri, L. Hughes, E. L. Slade, A. Jeyaraj, A. K. Kar, R. Wright (2023). Opinion paper: 'So what if ChatGPT wrote it?' Multidisciplinary perspectives on opportunities, challenges and implications of generative conversational AI for research, practice and policy. *International Journal of Information Management*, 71, 102642. https://doi.org/10.1016/j.ijinfomgt:.2023.102642.

Farrokhnia, M., S. K. Banihashem, O. Noroozi, & A. Wals (2023). A SWOT analysis of ChatGPT: Implications for educational practice and research. *Innovations in Education and Teaching International*, 61(3), 460–474. https://doi.org/10.1080/14703297.2023.2195846.

Fryer, L. K., D. Coniam, R. Carpenter, & D. Lăpușneanu (2020). Bots for language learning now: Current and future directions. *Language, Learning and Technology*, 24(2), 8–22.

Fui-Hoon Nah, F., R. Zheng, J. Cai, K. Siau, & L. Chen (2023). Generative AI and ChatGPT: Applications, challenges, and AI-human collaboration. *Journal of Information Technology Case and Application Research*, 25(3), 277–304.

Godwin-Jones, R. (2022). Partnering with AI: Intelligent writing assistance and instructed language learning. *Language Learning & Technology*, 26(2), 5–24. http://doi.org/10125/73474.

Godwin-Jones, R. (2024). Distributed agency in second language learning and teaching through generative AI. *Language Learning & Technology*, 28(2), 5–30. https://doi.org/10125/73570.

Gruber, P. (2023) Using ChatGPT for efficient data analysis with R. *Instats Inc*. https://doi.org/10.61700/XWWIQWCMK4X0R469.

Harmer, J. (2015). *The Practice of English Language Teaching*. Pearson.

Hockly. N. (2023). Artificial intelligence in English language teaching: The good, the bad and the ugly. *RELC Journal*, 54(2): 445–451. https://doi.org/10.1177/00336882231168504.

Hong, W. C. H. (2023). The impact of ChatGPT on foreign language teaching and learning: Opportunities in education and research. *Journal of Educational Technology and Innovation*, 5(1), 37–45. https://jeti.thewsu.org/index.php/cieti/article/view/103.

Instefjord, E. J., & E. Munthe (2017). Educating digitally competent teachers: A study of integration of professional digital competence in teacher education. *Teaching and Teacher Education*, 67, 37–45.

Jacobs, H. H., & M. Fisher (2023). *Prompt literacy: A key for AI-based learning*. www.ascd.org/el/articles/prompt-literacy-a-key-for-ai-based-learning.

Javier, D. R. C., & B. L. Moorhouse (2023). Developing secondary school English language learners' productive and critical use of ChatGPT. *TESOL Journal*, (e755), 1–9.

Jeon, J., & S. Lee (2023). Large language models in education: A focus on the complementary relationship between human teachers and ChatGPT. *Education and Information Technologies*, 28, 5873–15892. https://doi.org/10.1007/s10639-023-11834-1.

Kasneci, E., K. Seßler, S. Küchemann, M. Bannert, D. Dementieva, F. Fischer, & G. Kasneci (2023). ChatGPT for good? On opportunities and challenges of large language models for education. *Learning and Individual Differences*, 103, 102274.

Kerr, P. (2014). *Translation and Own-Language Activities*. Cambridge University Press.

Knoth, N., A. Tolzin, & A. Janson (2024). AI literacy and its implications for prompt engineering strategies. *Computers and Education: Artificial Intelligence*, 49(4), 100225. https://doi.org/10.1016/j.caeai.2024.100225.

Kohnke, L. (2023). *Using Technology to Design ESL/EFL Microlearning Activities*. Springer.

Kohnke, L., & A. Jarvis (2023). Developing infographics for English for academic purposes courses. *TESOL Journal*, 14, e675. https://doi.org/10.1002/tesj.6753-197.

Kohnke, L., D. Foung, & D. Zou (2024). Microlearning: A new normal for flexible teacher professional development in online and blended learning. *Education and Information Technologies*, 29(4), 4457–4480.

Kohnke, L., D. Foung, D. Zou, & M. Jiang (2024). Creating the conditions for professional digital competence through microlearning. *Educational Technology & Society*, 27(1), 18.

Kohnke, L., & B. L. Moorhouse (2024). An exploration of microlearning as continuous professional development for English language teachers: Initial findings and insights. *Open Learning: The Journal of Open, Distance and e-Learning*, 1–17.

Kohnke, L., B. L. Moorhouse, & D. Zou (2023). Using ChatGPT for language teaching and learning. *RELC Journal*, 54(2), 537–550. https://doi.org/10.1177/00336882231162868.

Kohnke, L. & D. Zou (2024). The role of ChatGPT in enhancing English teaching: A paradigm shift in lesson planning and instructional practice. *Educational Technology and Society*, 28(3), 4–20.

König, J., D. J. Jäger-Biela, & N. Glutsch (2020). Adapting to online teaching during Covid-19 school closure: Teacher education and teacher competence effects among early career teachers in Germany. *European Journal of Teacher Education*, 43(4), 608–622.

Kostka, I., & R. Toncelli (2023). Exploring applications of ChatGPT to English language teaching: Opportunities, challenges, and recommendations. *Teaching English as a Second or Foreign Language*, 27(3). https://doi.org/10.55593/ej.27107int.

Lee, Y. J. (2020). The long-term effect of automated writing evaluation feedback on writing development. *English Teaching*, 75(1), 67–92.

Lee, S., & J. Jeon (2024). Enhancing pre-service EFL teachers' TPACK through chatbot-integrated lesson planning projects. *Language Learning & Technology*, 28(1), 1–20. https://hdl.handle.net/10125/73598.

Lim, W. M., A. Gunasekara, J. L. Pallant, J. I. Pallant, & E. Pechenkina (2023). Generative AI and the future of education: Ragnarök or reformation? A paradoxical perspective from management educators. *International Journal of Management in Education*, 21(2), 100790. https://doi.org/10.1016/j.ijme.2023.100790.

Lo, L. S. (2023). The CLEAR path: A framework for enhancing information literacy through prompt engineering. *The Journal of Academic Librarianship*, 49(4), 102720. https://doi.org/10.1016/j.acalib.2023.102720.

Lucchi, N. (2023). ChatGPT: A case study on copyright challenges for generative artificial intelligence systems. *European Journal of Risk Regulation*, 1–23. https://doi.org/10.1017/err.2023.59.

Lund, B. D., T. Wang, N. R. Mannuru, B. Nie, S. Shimray, & Z. Wang (2023). ChatGPT and a new academic reality: Artificial intelligence-written research papers and the ethics of the large language models in scholarly publishing. *Journal of the Association for Information Science and Technology*, 74(5), 570–581. https://doi.org/10.1002/asi.24750.

Maloy, R. W., & S. Gattupalli (2024). Prompt literacy. *EdTechnica*, https://doi.org/10.59668/371.14442.

McGrath, I. (2016). *Materials Evaluation and Design for Language Teaching*. Edinburgh University Press.

Meniado, J. C. (2023). Digital language teaching 5.0: Technologies, trends and competencies. *RELC Journal*, 54(2), 461–473.

Milroy, J. (2001). Language ideologies and the consequences of standardization. *Journal of Sociolinguistics*, 5(4), 530–555. https://doi.org/10.1111/1467-9481.00163.

Mishan, F. (2015). *Materials Development for TESOL*. Edinburgh University Press.

Mishra, P., M. Warr, & R. Islam (2023). TPACK in the age of ChatGPT and generative AI. *Journal of Digital Learning in Teacher Education*, 39(4), 235–251. http://dx.doi.org/10.1080/21532974.2023.2247480.

Mizumoto, A., & M. Eguchi (2023). Exploring the potential of using an AI language model for automated essay scoring. *Research Methods in Applied Linguistics*, 2(2), 100050. https://doi.org/10.1016/j.rmal.2023.100050.

Moorhouse, B. L. (2023). Teachers' digital technology use after a period of online teaching. *ELT Journal*, 77(4), 445–457.

Moorhouse, B. L. (2024). Generative artificial intelligence and ELT. *ELT Journal*, 78(4), 378–392. https://doi.org/10.1093/elt/ccae032.

Moorhouse, B. L., T. Y. Ho, C. Wu, & Y. Wan (2025). Pre-service language teachers' task-specific large language model prompting practices. *RELC Journal*. https://doi.org/10.1177/00336882251313701.

Moorhouse, B. L., & L. Kohnke (2024). The effects of generative AI on initial language teacher education: The perceptions of teacher educators. *System*, 122, 103290. https://doi.org/10.1016/j.system.2024.103290.

Moorhouse, B. L., Y. Wan, T. Y. Ho, & A. M. Lin (2024). Generative AI-assisted, evidence-informed use of L1 in L2 classrooms. *ELT Journal*, 78(4), 453–465.

Moorhouse, B. L., K. M. Wong, & L. Li (2023). Teaching with technology in the post-pandemic digital age: Technological normalisation and AI-induced disruptions. *RELC Journal*, 54(2), 311–320. https://doi.org/10.1177/00336882231176929.

Moorhouse, B. L., & L. Yan (2023). Use of digital tools by English language schoolteachers. *Education Sciences*, 13(3), 226.

Ng, D. T. K., J. K. L. Leung, J. Su, R. C. W. Ng, & S. K. W. Chu (2023). Teachers' AI digital competencies and twenty-first century skills in the post-pandemic world. *Educational Technology Research & Development*, 71(1), 137–161.

Palfreyman, D. M., & P. Benson (2019). Autonomy and its role in English language learning: Practice and research. In *Second Handbook of English Language Teaching*, X. Gao, editor. Springer, 661–681.

Pinter, A. (2017). *Teaching Young Language Learners*. Oxford University Press.

Porter, B., & E. Machery (2024) AI-generated poetry is indistinguishable from human-written poetry and is rated more favorably. *Scientific Reports*, 14, 26133. https://doi.org/10.1038/s41598-024-76900-1.

Reinhardt, K. S., & S. Elwood (2019). Promising practices in online training and support: Microlearning and personal learning environments to promote a growth mindset in learners. In *Handbook of Research on Virtual Training and Mentoring of Online Instructors*, 298–310. IGI Global.

Richards, J. C. (2010). Competence and performance in language teaching. *RELC Journal*, 41(2), 101–122. https://doi.org/10.1177/0033688210372953.

Richards, J. C. (2015). Materials design in language teacher education: An example from Southeast Asia. In *International Perspectives on English Language Teacher Education: Innovations from the Field*, 90–106. Palgrave Macmillan UK.

Richards, J. C., & T. S. Rodgers (2014). *Approaches and Methods in Language Teaching (Third Edition)*. Cambridge University Press.

Rifkin, B. (2003). Oral proficiency learning outcomes and curricular design. *Foreign Language Annals*, 36(4), 582–588.

Scarino, A. (2009). Assessing intercultural capability in learning languages: Some issues and considerations. *Language Teaching*, 42, 67–80. https://doi.org/10.1017/S0261444808005417.

Scrivener, J. (2011). *Learning Teaching*. Macmillan.

Shaikh, S., S. M. Daudpota, S. Y. Yayilgan, & S. Sindhu (2023). Exploring the potential of large-language models (LLMs) for student feedback sentiment analysis. In *2023 International Conference on Frontiers of Information Technology (FIT)*, 214–219. Institute of Electrical and Electronics Engineers.

Shin, D., & J. H. Lee (2023). Can ChatGPT make reading comprehension testing items on par with human experts? *Language Learning & Technology*, 27(3), 27–40.

Smith, G., E. Fleisig, M. Bossi, I. Rustagi, & X. Yin (2024). Standard language ideology in AI-generated language. *arXiv*, arXiv:2406.08726.

Speechace (2024). Speaking test. *Speechace*. www.speechace.com/speaking-test/.

Stahl, B. C., & D. Eke (2024). The ethics of ChatGPT: Exploring the ethical issues of an emerging technology. *International Journal of Information Management*, 74, 102700. https://doi.org/10.1016/j.ijinfomgt.2023.102700.

Steiss, J., T. Tate, S. Graham, J. Cruz, M. Hebert, J. Wang, & C. B. Olson (2024). Comparing the quality of human and ChatGPT feedback of students' writing. *Learning and Instruction*, 91, 101894.

Stockwell, G., & Y. Wang (2023). Exploring the challenges of technology in language teaching in the aftermath of the pandemic. *RELC Journal*, 54(2), 474–482. https://doi.org/10.1177/00336882231168438.

Stockwell, G., & Y. Wang (2024). Expanding the learning ecology and autonomy of language learners with mobile technologies. *Educational Technology and Society*, 27(2), 60–69. https://doi.org/10.30191/ETS.202404_27(2).SP05.

Strokel-Walker, C. (2024, May 1). AI chatbots have thoroughly infiltrated scientific publishing. *Scientific American*. www.scientificamerican.com/article/chatbots-have-thoroughly-infiltrated-scientific-publishing/.

Thornbury, S. (1999). *How to Teach Grammar*. Longman

Thorne, S. L. (2003). Artifacts and cultures-of-use in intercultural communication. *Language Learning & Technology*, 7(2), 38–67. http://llt.msu.edu/vol7num2/thorne/.

Tomlinson, B. (2014). 7 teacher growth through materials development. *The European Journal of Applied Linguistics and TEFL*, 3(2), 89–107.

Tomlinson, B. (2015). Developing principled materials for young learners of English as a foreign. In *Teaching English to Young Learners: Critical Issues in Language Teaching with 3-12 Year Olds*, J. Bland, editor. Bloomsbury, 279.

Trust, T. (2023). Essential considerations for addressing the possibility of AI-driven cheating, part 2. www.facultyfocus.com/articles/teaching-with-technology-articles/essential-considerations-for-addressing-the-possibility-of-ai-driven-cheating-part-2/.

Tseng, W., & M. Warschauer (2023). AI-writing tools in education: If you can't beat them, join them. *Journal of China Computer-Assisted Language Learning*, 3(2), 258–262.

van den Berg, G. & E. du Plessis (2023). ChatGPT and generative AI: Possibilities for its contribution to lesson planning, critical thinking and openness in teacher education. *Education Sciences*, 13(10), 998. https://doi.org/10.3390/educsci13100998.

Walters, W. H., & E. I. Wilder (2023). Fabrication and errors in the bibliographic citations generated by ChatGPT. *Scientific Reports*, 13(1), 14045. https://doi.org/10.1038/s41598-023-41032-5.

Wan, Y., & B. L. Moorhouse (2024). Using Call Annie as a generative artificial intelligence speaking partner for language learners. *RELC Journal*. https://doi.org/10.1177/00336882231224813.

Wang, L., X. Chen, X. Deng, H. Wen, M. You, W. Liu, Q. Li, & J. Li (2024). Prompt engineering in consistency and reliability with the evidence-based guideline for LLMs. *npj Digital Medicine*, 7, 41. https://doi.org/10.1038/s41746-024-01029-4.

Warschauer, M., W. Tseng, S. Yim, T. Webster, S. Jacob, Q. Du, & T. Tate (2023). The affordances and contradictions of AI-generated text for writers of English as a second or foreign language. *Journal of Second Language Writing*. https://doi.org/10.2139/ssrn.4404380.

Yeo, M. A., B. L. Moorhouse, & Y. Wan (2025). From academic text to talk-show: Deepening engagement and understanding with Google NotebookLM. *TESL-EJ*, 28(4), 1–14.

Zhang, R., & D. Zou (2024). Self-regulated second language learning: A review of types and benefits of strategies, modes of teacher support, and pedagogical implications. *Computer Assisted Language Learning*, 37(4), 720–765.

Cambridge Elements

Generative AI in Education

Mark Warschauer
University of California, Irvine

Mark Warschauer is a Distinguished Professor of Education at the University of California, with affiliated faculty appointments in the Departments of Informatics, Language Science, and Psychological Science. He is a member of the National Academy of Education and the director of the UCI Digital Learning Lab. Professor Warschauer is one of the most influential scholars in the world on digital learning, digital literacy, and the US of AI in Education. He has published 12 books on these topics including with MIT Press, Cambridge University Press, Teachers College Press, and Yale University Press, and some 300 scientific articles and papers. His work has been cited more than 48,000 times, making him one of the most cited researchers in the world on educational technology. He previously served as founding editor of Language Learning & Technology and inaugural editor of AERA Open.

Tamara Tate
University of California, Irvine

Tamara Tate is a Project Scientist at the University of California, Irvine, and Associate Director of the Digital Learning Lab. She leads the Lab's work on digital and online tools to support teaching and learning including generative AI, partnering with school districts, universities, nonprofit organizations, media and tech developers, and others in iterative development and evaluation. As the PI of a NSF-funded grant, she is studying the use of generative AI in undergraduate writing courses. She also studies secondary student writing as a member of the IES-funded national WRITE Center. She received her B.A. in English and her Ph.D. in Education at U.C. Irvine and her J.D. at U.C. Berkeley.

Editorial Board

Stephen Aguilar, *University of Southern California, US*
Maha Bali, *American University in Cairo, Egypt*
Irene-Angelica Chounta, *University of Duisburg-Essen, Germany*
Shayan Doroudi, *University of California, Irvine, US*
María Florencia Ripani, *Ceibal Foundation, Uruguay*
Bart Rientes, *The Open University, UK*
Neil Selwyn, *Monash University, Australia*
Jiahong Su, *The University of Hong Kong*
Ulrich Trautwein, *University of Tübingen, Germany*
Ying Xu, *Harvard University*

About the Series

Generative AI is one of the most disruptive technologies in modern history, with the potential to dramatically transform education for better or worse. This series will address cutting-edge topics on the intersection of generative AI with educational research and practice for diverse learners from early childhood to adult.

Cambridge Elements⹀

Generative AI in Education

Elements in the Series

Generative AI in Computer Science Education
Diana Franklin, Paul Denny, David A. Gonzalez-Maldonado and Minh Tran

Generative Artificial Intelligence and Language Teaching
Benjamin Luke Moorhouse and Kevin M. Wong

A full series listing is available at: www.cambridge.org/EAIE

For EU product safety concerns, contact us at Calle de José Abascal, 56–1º,
28003 Madrid, Spain or eugpsr@cambridge.org.

www.ingramcontent.com/pod-product-compliance
Ingram Content Group UK Ltd.
Pitfield, Milton Keynes, MK11 3LW, UK
UKHW022047110326
468905UK00021B/2475